John Mitchell, Marion Juliet Mitchell

The Poetical works of John Mitchell

John Mitchell, Marion Juliet Mitchell

The Poetical works of John Mitchell

ISBN/EAN: 9783743308701

Manufactured in Europe, USA, Canada, Australia, Japa

Cover: Foto ©Thomas Meinert / pixelio.de

Manufactured and distributed by brebook publishing software (www.brebook.com)

John Mitchell, Marion Juliet Mitchell

The Poetical works of John Mitchell

THE
POETICAL WORKS

JOHN MITCHELL, M.D.

CHICAGO:
SHEPARD & JOHNSTON, PRINTERS.
1883.

PROEM.

Since many a pilgrim up Parnassus plods
His way, to reach its airy peak, and fails—
Perhaps, because of wanting power innate,
A requisite that cannot be acquired—
Far up the dizzy height I dare not climb;
Lest haply I should fall, and if unscathed,
Must needs, till spent, a hopeless life endure
In truceless discontent, and with the rest,
The pity of the wise, and scoff of fools.

Nor would I envy him who finds his name
Within the Temple, on the roll of fame,
If at the cost of social earthly joys,
Continuous toil, and hope deferred until
The world's applause, that wakes him from his dream,
Shall be the prelude of his parting years.

Far better would it be, through life to toil,
And hazard brave, to reach the prize and fail,
Than live a life of sensuality,
And like a pampered brute forgotten die.

Aye, though his aim be crossed, and labor lost,
And he depart unpitied and unsung,
Still nobly shall he have his duty done.

When virtuous passions are predominant,
Ambition is a laudable desire,
An aspiration of the restless soul
To rise above material decay
And solve the problem of its destiny!

Annihilation! shade of consciousness!
I shudder at thy dark and endless Night!
The fathomless, unknowable Abyss!

Whomsoever would his fellows serve,
In whatsoever sphere allotted him,
That his own life should not be vainly spent,
If faithful, cherishes a hope to live,
In kind remembrance through the lapse of time;
And should he earn the meed, begrudge it not,
For with its aid he might some soul improve.

In store for me, then, may there be reserved,
Upon the ladder of fame, a lowly round,
Where I can find immunity from care,
At peace with all, and envious of none,
Unruffled watching the numbered sands of life,
Softly fall adown the hour-glass;
Then when the process ends, will kindred souls,
Who in his weal rejoiced, and wept his woe,
Appreciate this token from a friend,
Whose lucubrations, for their welfare meet,
Oft toiled to render, during leisure hours;
And if to their behoof the tribute prove,
His life and toil shall not have been in vain.

CONTENTS.

	PAGE
PROEM	3
YOUTH'S SWEET MORNING DREAMS	7
IT CALLS TO MIND	9
FRIENDLY SMILES AND VOICES	11
PHILIP BLAINE	12
THE REBELLION	15
SOLITUDE	18
THE RECLUSE OF THE HUT IN THE DELL	21
PARAPHRASE ON THE LAST CHAPTER OF ECCLESIASTES	35
DISCONTENT	36
HADES	38
WILLIAM AND RUTH	40
THE OLD OAK TREE	44
MAN WAS NOT MADE TO MOURN	68
WINTRY NIGHT	69
ROCK RIVER	72
THE VILLAGE BELLE	75
THE TWINKLING STAR	77
THE EXILE	97
THE SEASONS	99
MORNING DREAM	101
HOEING THE GARDEN	104
THE REIGN OF TERROR	106
VICISSITUDES	116
ALL AT HOME	118
ON THE DEATH OF J. C.	123
THE VANISHED YEAR	125
THE INDIAN'S DOOM	127
THE STUDENT'S MIDNIGHT MONOLOGUE	145

	PAGE
DREAM OF LIFE	146
JEMMY MCFARLING	148
RESTLESS THOUGHTS	152
SWEET CHILDHOOD	153
EUGENE WADE	155
THE LIGHT OF THE PAST	172
INGLESIDE	175
THE WATCHER'S RAMBLE	177
CRITIQUE OF BYRON'S ODE TO NAPOLEON	180
THE MIRROR OF LIFE	188
TO THE MEMORY OF J. B. M.	190
NEAR THE SHORE	191
MY CHILDHOOD'S OLD HOME IN THE VALLEY	193

POEMS BY MARION MITCHELL

HOURS OF THE PAST	205
A MODERN WEDDING	207
MY GRANDMOTHER'S HOME	210
AN EVENING SCENE	212
POETIC PURITY	214
THE STORY OF A LIFE	215
TO BRITAIN'S NOBLE QUEEN	218
WAITING	220
THE OLD HERMIT	221
PASSING AWAY	224
A REVERY	225
TO MY FATHER ON HIS EIGHTIETH BIRTHDAY	226
THE VILLAGE CHURCH	228
OLD MUSIC	231
TO LITTLE MAY MCCORMICK	232
THE RETURN OF THE ROBIN	233
THE DYING CHILD	235
OLD OCEAN	237
SOMEBODY	238
ACROSTICS	239

THE POETICAL WORKS

OF

JOHN MITCHELL, M.D.

YOUTH'S SWEET MORNING DREAMS.

There are no joys the Fount bestows,
    In pure and lulling streams,
That sweeten life and soothe its woes,
    Like youth's sweet morning dreams.

We up the hill eventful soar,
    Thereon to cares betake us;
There our vanished joys dream o'er,
    And still they happy make us.

Though sometimes troubled are a few,
    And dark our way appears,
With vigor braced, we ills subdue,
    And tranquilize our fears.

While Fancy over youth bears sway,
    None sweeter e'er come o'er us
Than of joys that deck our way,
    Till bright it looks before us.

We some of these leave on the hill,
    Mong others the way adorned;
And all asleep repeated still:
    Awake are ever mourned.

Our groping down the slope denied
    Of strength, doth oft remind us,—
On the crown and sunny-side,
    We left our joys behind us.

And as we from them journey on,
    In revery often hear,
The hill o'er which we shall have gone,
    Reverberate their cheer.

And till we reach the foot, and passed
    Are all the days assigned us,
Our sweetest dreams are first and last
    Of joys we leave behind us.

IT CALLS TO MIND.

When heedful housewives needles ply,
And wild-geese soar on pinions high,
    To reach a genial clime,
It calls to mind: they wisdom teach,
That men oft fail to learn, who reach
    To compass the sublime.

When frosts have nipt the leaves and flowers,
And withered are the viny bowers,
    Erewhile in fruit abounding,
It calls to mind : my youthful days,
Their innocent, sweetening rounds of plays,
    And sweets with gall redounding.

When trees stand trembling in the blast,
That off their foliage have cast,
    And strewed the earth beneath,
It calls to mind: th' return of May,
Its budding, blooming rosary,
    The nosegay and the wreath.

When shrill and loud the tempests roar,
Congealed the pond, or but the shore
    Ice-bound, as with a girth,
It calls to mind: the fire will glare,
In due time on some dear one's chair,
    Left vacant on the hearth.

When husbandmen have slaughtered swine,
Their garners filled and housed their kine,
    And from their toil repose,
It calls to mind: my mission here,
To answer for with life's career,
    Is drawing to a close.

When nursery-tales the matrons tell,
And requiems sing, and curfews knell,
    O man, their sayings learn
And heed: "Moulded thou art from clay,
And perishable, needs pass away,
    And unto earth return."

When winter, weary earth below,
In drapery wraps of feathery snow,
    Fitting for her rest,
It calls to mind: as by the fire
I muse, she will in new attire,
    Again be richly dressed.

FRIENDLY SMILES AND VOICES.

When not a sigh a bosom rends,
    At home, the fire beside :
There in the voices of our friends,
    Is music the even-tide.

How sweet the voices are of friends,
    At home, as it we near :
And each one's ready welcome tends
    To ever it endear.

There's nothing like the smile of friends,
    To stir the heart aglow :
Till tingling to the finger's ends,
    Its blood is felt to flow.

How sweet the voices are of friends,
    When at the door they meet us :
As each one a hand extends,
    And altogether greet us.

Sweet home at eve, and kindred friends,
    With faces smiling cheery,
For the worry of day, amends
    Sufficient make the weary.

PHILIP BLAINE.

Long since had ceased the cannon's roar,
   The clang of arms and trumpets stilled;
   The wounded, yet among the killed,
Were lying in their freezing gore.

The moon her visage wan revealed,
   The stars around her twinkling bright;
   And all were keeping watch that night,
O'er Lookout Mountain's battle-field.

A youth, with many a veteran old,
   Lay weltering in his blood still flowing;
   And though bleak the blast was blowing —
He suffered more from fear than cold:

Lest, to stanch the blood, due aid
   Should come too late, he having plied
   The means he had till laid aside:
Nor end attained, nor progress made.

Philip, for the war had left,
   Clandestinely, his Mother lorn;
   And day and night did often mourn,
She by him was of peace bereft.

To the conviction left, of all
   The sorest: that which comes too late,
   He owned the justice of his fate,
And more, he felt it past recall.

So, trembling lay, in dripping gore,
   The Mother's hope and only joy;
   She trembled too, but for her boy,
As she had heard the cannons roar.

He thought of home, and with a sigh;
   But as soft echo answer made,
   Hope whispered, "It is timely aid,
That greets thee with a sweet reply."

Yet soon the light of Hope was hid,
   And echo spent in sighing wind;
   He deemed from friends he left behind,
All aid and comfort were forbid.

Despondent, but exhausted more,
   He swooned, but soon revived and slept;
   And dreamt his Mother o'er him wept,
As she full oft had done before:

When she could not resist his cry,
   But caught and clasped him to her breast,
   With love maternal him caressed,
And sweetly sung her lullaby.

Ere long his happy dream was past:
   He woke with pain in murky night;
   The moon and stars refused their light,
And chilly blew the northern blast.

Waiting his doom, prepared to meet,
  He thought he heard another sigh:
  For that of th' wind it seemed too nigh,
And brought a thrill of joy too sweet.

Once more he looked for timely aid,
  Again Hope cheered his drooping heart;
  When, closed the wound, he felt the smart—
His Mother's hand was on it laid.

For she had followed in the rear,
  While on his march, her darling child;
  And, till it closed, the battle wild,
Without his ken, she watched in fear.

And when the din of strife had ceased,
  To the encampment she retired,
  By a Mother's hope inspired,
Dwindling as her fears increased.

She many knew who loved her well;
  For tidings these did she accost:
  All feared that her poor boy was lost,
But of their fears declined to tell.

Maternal love, true to the last,
  Sustained her heart when hope was fled;
  Back to the field she quickly sped,
Whereon the tragic scene had passed.

She found him lying 'mong the slain,
   Where wildest raged the mortal strife ;
   And kindl'd with love, a spark of life,
Fitfully glimmering in its wane.

THE REBELLION.

When brotherly love and morals are on the wane,
And ruthless men all sacred things profane,
And when uncurbed their vicious passions rage
And war they 'gainst their native country wage,
And laws by their forefathers made do break,
And all the loyal cherish is at stake,
And Ignorance wise precepts disobeys,
And mad Fanaticism reason sways:
An agent on a mission from above,
'Twould seem, is sometimes sent below in love,
With powers equal to th' emergence given,
To fulfil the high behest of Heaven.

In times eventful, men immortal rise,
Who could not be immortal otherwise;
Some in the highest sphere of life are sought,
While others from obscurity are brought ;

Yet come they will, already with a name,
Or one to win, or earn, and leave to fame;
And those who shone with lustre bright before,
By these may be eclipsed and shine no more.

There sometimes may be more than one required,
Whose souls with zeal are for their errand fired;
In this case that all christendom concerned,
There requisite were three, who well discerned
Its magnitude, with aptitude, 'twould seem,
Commensurate, and all of high esteem:
Lincoln first, and Seward second place,
And Douglas last, a trust nor least to grace,
Nor less hard than of either's to endure;
As firm in what was just, in trust as sure,
He his fulfilled and dignified as well,
Till, spent his strength, he 'neath his burden fell.

But that event, inscrutable to all,
Had not yet come, that all must needs befall;
First in their order others needs transpire,
Which coming brought withal a hydra dire.

Still that in olden time of sin begot,
 Nor that which Hercules did his strength employ,
  At times, in duteous conflict to destroy,
Is not the one whereof I treat and wot.
This is the monster Treason, that in mien
More fearful is, than any ever seen;
In ancient days or nights, begot of sin,
Or since, mayhap, of all its kith and kin.

It came from th' east, like many another pest,
With stealthy pace, to devastate the west;
At Charleston it its first appearance made,
And there in conclave with abettors stayed;
Wherewith had Jackson been unable to cope
By other means, he would have used a rope;
A hint thereof alarmed the subtle foe,
And mightiest, too, of Freedom here below;
And still unhung, it to its lair withdrew,
To brood o'er plots, and plot again perdu.

A calm ensued! as in midsummer warm,
Serene and bland, it oft forebodes a storm;
And time still lapsed, and still the world turned round
Upon its axis, by its orbit bound,
Wherein, as coming events in turn drew near,
Its peoples waiting, watched with hope and fear.

Anon the scene was changed! the storm drew nigh,
Darkening, as it came, both earth and sky!
Again the monster from its lair arose,
Like Banquo's ghost, that could not find repose;
And though events that must needs pass had passed.
And culminated in the greatest last,
His part therein had done, he took to do,
And yet knew not he rendered aid thereto.
Now in his zenith Douglas reappeared,
To save fair Freedom from the foe she feared.
Her able-bodied host therefor were all
From every source found needful at her call;

And with that unforgotten faithful host
None else could bring, his heart and soul engrossed
In his prime aim, that of his country's weal,
He to the rescue came with ardent zeal.

The end was peace! wherein he rendered aid!
How much, when justly in the balance weighed,
Time shall reveal and history record!
The world will render merit meet reward,—
And howso long deferred, another name
Will surely be enrolled, and left to fame;
And yet fair Freedom's foe, her only dread,
Once more to plots hatch, to its refuge fled—
The many-headed Monster was not dead.

SOLITUDE.

O solitude serene and sweet!
In some lone favorite retreat,
Whereso thou art, fain would I be,
To by thy converse learn of thee
The peaceful and delightful way
Of wisdom, and her voice obey.

Is there on earth a light that glows,
Except what Heaven alone bestows,
And that beams on the pilgrim's way
So clear he need not go astray?

In search of light, a fruitful theme
I found, "which was not all a dream!"
Save thee mine intimate, forlorn
I left my study in the morn
And rambled 'mong the scenes of Spring,
Where merry-winged warblers sing,
And flowers bloom, and zephyrs bear
Their dulcet odors through the air,
And Summer scenes, where husbandmen
Were harvesting their crops again
In bright or sultry midday hours,
Morning dews and evening showers.

When all those charming scenes were passed,
I one of Nature reached at last,
Her countenance was still sublime,
Because she yet was in her prime;
The birds sang on the boughs of trees,
That still waved in an August breeze;
And still the foliage was green,
And 'twas of all the fairest scene.

On her unruffled mien I dwelt
With joy till fled, and sorrow felt,
As restless thought took wider range,
In view of all the coming change
That soon therein must needs ensue,
From gay, to grave with sombrous hue.

I laid me down upon her lap—
Because of weariness, mayhap,
Of powers put to truceless strain —
Tranquillity and light to gain.

While on her breast I leant my head,
Mine old companion softly said :
" Here Nature speaks in language fit,
Alone, to glimmering light emit !
Yet with what suns and moons bestow,
And that wherewith the stars all glow,
Is what he needs who aims at more,
With fortitude a height to soar
Worthy of an immortal soul,
Aspiring to a glorious goal ;
Albeit all do not reveal
The sum thereof, they naught conceal !"
Wherewith did happily conclude
My colloquy with Solitude.

THE RECLUSE OF THE HUT IN THE DELL.

The curfew ceased tolling when, over the lea
And up the wild vale of the lone Tennessee,
Afar from my home and its joys had I wended,
Ere th' moon 'neath the western horizon descended.

Nor broken the silence, nor wakened a thrill,
Save by the sad cry of the lorn whippoorwill,
Or creaking of boughs interwove, as the trees
To and fro gently swayed in the summer night's breeze.

Lured on by these pleasures to others more dear,
My course I pursued through the wilderness drear;
Though rarely the heavens afforded a ray
To point out my lonely and tortuous way

At length the tall cliff, and my object attained,
Its steep mounted up, and its proud summit gained,
In climbing aweary, I there sat me down
On the moss covered rock that it wore as a crown.

By day had I here often sought Nature's charms,
But now in the night was embraced in her arms;
She reigned in her primitive grandeur and grace,
And charming because of no change in her face.

Around me the forest spread out its dark shade,
And lulling the sound that the breeze through it made;
Beneath me a chasm, and wound round the hill,
As the moon shimmered on it, a murmuring rill.

While there on the rock I sat gazing around
On the beautiful picture, in silence profound,
In the wold, with a visage careworn, I espied
A grave, hoary man, with his hound by his side.

A change in the scene his appearance had brought,
And as sudden a turn to the current of thought;
At fault was conjecture, till soon it appeared
He was there to commune with his God whom he feared.

Uncovered he stood, like a church-going saint,
With reverence meet, though his language was quaint;
As blended with pity was scorn toward man,
In the suit he thus urged, so devoutly began:

"When man in the garden of Eden did dwell,
Ere Satan deceived him, and from grace he fell,
As the gigantic oak is the king of the wood,
The noblest of creatures—a monarch he stood.

"But mutable now, as became Aaron's rod,
A change hath come over that image of God;
Than man a foe greater, man hath not to fear,
Pride, malice, and envy, all mark his career.

"Yet, Father, forgive all my sins against Thee,
And others from further reproach will I free;
Oh, take my poor spirit, in thine own due time,
To mansions eternal, supernal, sublime!"

His prayer having ended, he left in the gloom
Of Night,—who her silence profound did resume,—
For the moon had just set, but aroused my concern
In his fate, I determined to more of him learn.

Having carefully marked the direction he took,
His hut I soon found in a bend of the brook;
The door was ajar, and a taper's dim light
Presented a comfortless, pitiful sight.

After twice gently knocking, he bade me "walk in,"
When, the greeting I met with that friendship doth win;
"Thou art welcome," said he, "to the hut in the dell,
Yet, wherefore thy visit, I beg thee to tell?"

I replied, "Gentle sir, I have seen thee in grief,
And in sympathy come, though it fail of relief;
Yet the tribute accept, and I naught will conceal
If thou in return wilt thy story reveal."

He sighed, but at once to my offer agreed;
Leant his head on his staff and then bade me proceed;
Complacently through my adventure he heard,
While notably anxious he weighed every word.

As I paused, he rejoined,—"Though sad be my tale,
To reciter or hearer, yet it may avail
To satisfy others, that due retribution
On earth for their deeds is an empty delusion.

"Bright season of childhood, fond memory's sweet dream,
The fount pure and tranquil of life's fitful stream!
Yet calmer and clearer and sweeter, we find,
It appears, as the farther we leave it behind.

"On the hey-day of youth, with events that befell
During its happy stage, it is pleasing to dwell;
O'er the visage of age it oft brings back a smile,
And with its bright scenes its dull time may beguile.

"But the charm passed away! and life's driving storm
The blood chilled in manhood that youth had kept warm;
I endeavored to stem it, but ere it was o'er
My ill-fated bark was a wreck on the shore.

"Ere legal construction pronounced me of age,
I hopefully entered on life's busy stage;
Whose scenes with delight seemed to o'er it abound,
And fruition thereof here below might be found.

"With a promising future yet buoyant and gay,
Auspicious the day-star arose on my way;
Nor dispirited e'en though it clouded became,
Nor relaxed were my efforts to compass my aim.

"In my prime; by the lure of her worth, I was led
One of Eve's fairest daughters and rarest to wed:
As then I believed, and thereafter the few
Happy years we together lived, proved it was true.

"But Death, in whom pity ne'er wakens a sigh,
Untimely and ruthlessly severed the tie,
In my rude cot then I, of my chief joy bereft,
As years lapsed, in sorrow forsaken was left.

"Yet time, the sole balm that brings radical cure
To the ailments of mind which frail mortals endure,
Mine own tranquilized, and propitious once more
Heaven graciously brought joy and peace to my door.

"While musing, as wont, on the bank of a stream,
That near by it flowed, I was roused from my dream,
By a cry for relief from a skiff tempest tost,
Lest it be, as construed, with its rich lading lost.

"Clinging fast to its stem sat a charming young maid,
At its stern, her own brother a stripling unstaid;
Too far had they ventured, when caught in a blast,
The sail to reduce that encumbered the mast,

"Which breaking soon, overboard with the lad fell,
Who, to save his own life, and his sister's as well,
Had it clung to, perhahs, wanting reason therefor,
And she was left lonely his loss to deplore.

"He having at once reached his goal and his grave;
And her from like fate it behooved me to save.
So thrilling her shrieks were, that rung through the air,
My manhood was challenged the danger to dare.

"And calling on Neptune his wrath to assuage,
I plunged in the water, still foaming with rage;
In a more fearful venture or perilous strife,
For his lady-love, knight never hazarded life.

"I, well nigh exhausted, the wreck at length gained,
Where the maid, well nigh lifeless, her place still maintained;
Unobserved I caught hold of the stern of the boat,
And turned its prow landward to thitherward float.

"My strength thus regaining, the time was but short
Ere the skiff I in safety had brought into port;
Nor long was it till to my hearth was conveyed
The drooping, bewildered and beautiful maid.

"The loss of her brother, exposure and fright,
Resulted in fever, and him to requite
Who came to the rescue, and long had watched o'er her,
Her hand she bestowed for the love that he bore her.

"Though Fortune relentlessly frowned in the main,
A few years of respite she spared us from pain;
And merciful Heaven vouchsafed us an heir,
Our allotment unknown, whatsoever, to share.

"But failing in commerce, by friends was I shunned,
By bailiffs annoyed and by creditors dunned;
And the prison, withal, of the debtor to flee,
For refuge my *dernier resort* was the sea.

"Confiding my darlings to one deemed my friend,
Whose wife was approaching an untimely end,
From a poor coffer's substance a pittance I drew,
And to all I held dear on the earth bade adieu.

"In an East India trader I traversed the oceans,
And visited marts where I trafficked in notions;
Till three thousand ducats I fairly did hoard,
For patient endurance a fitting reward.

"But like a sweet dream that on waking hath fled,
My riches took wing and away swiftly sped:
So Fortune with smiles, oft alluring, deceives us,
And with increased burdens in mockery leaves us.

"Beset with grim pirates, the pests of the sea,
Both treasure and freedom were lost unto me;
I drudging toil some sixteen years had pursued,
When the vilest of masters I chanced to elude.

"I landed upon the Atlantic's west shore,
As grateful to God as the pilgrims of yore;
The ills of the land more inclined to endure,
Than resort to the sea for the means of their cure.

"But my load-star that lit me with many a ray,
As it rose in my dreams, on my homeward-bound way,
From its orbit had wandered, and though in like sphere,
It revolved round another, with radiance clear.

"Yet the daughters of Eve, I would neither provoke,
Their virtues dishonor, nor blemishes cloak:
My wife long defended, while others inveighed me,
And would have proved faithful, had not he betrayed me

"In whom I confided, and who o'er and o'er,
Had craftily whispered that I was no more;
So was she torn from me, and severed the chain,
That never can here be united again.

"All doubts to dispel, and the truth realize,
To my cottage the rumor I traced in disguise:
My doom, the severest imposed upon mortal,
At once was confirmed when I entered its portal.

"As a cloud shades the landscape, some sad recollection,
Her brow seemed to dim, yet of peerless perfection;
It vanished anon, and though kind was her greeting,
Still wanting the whilom caresses, our meeting.

"Where once met with smiles that eclipsed its bright fires,
A stranger I sat at the hearth of my sires;
A group of fair children there gathered around me,
Of grief unaware that to secrecy bound me.

"Within an embrasure, and comely his look,
I observed a young man, who sat conning a book:
Mine own beloved son, whom I longed to embrace,
But Nature impulsive to prudence gave place.

"Overwhelmed with my fate, I ere long took my leave,
To hopelessly bear it without a reprieve;
And have borne it while roaming and in my retreat,
With the only friend left me — my dog at thy feet.

"Yet while I of fortune and hope am bereft,
There are other solaces unto me left:
My loved ones are sheltered where want is unknown!
And there in my rambles anights I am prone

"To watch o'er them keep, when they lie down to rest;
And the sweetest of all, is to know they are blest:
And while it affords me a pittance of pleasure,
Ungrateful 'twould be to repine at the measure.

"The Matron hath taciturn grown and depressed,
As if by a burden long borne in her breast,
She fain would find relief from, and could more or less,
Perhaps, should its cause she to some friend confess.

"Oft 'lone at the ingle till quenched is the blaze,
She broods o'er what surely must shorten her days;
But sad 'tis to dwell on a picture's dark side
Whose brightest nor nature nor patience can bide.

"Many ills have I borne, but succumbed to the last!
My days, long since numbered, all soon shall have passed;
The world I abandoned with its empty strife,
And here have retreated to close a vain life.

"Not unlike a lone exile in some sterile waste,
Forbidden forever all comfort to taste,
Where of life there no vestige appears on his way,
Not even so much as to mark its decay.

"If exacting in dealing with frail mortal man,
And as such, his actions too rigidly scan,
May Heaven forgive me wherein I offend,
And grant me the grace that I fail to extend.

"My story appears to have given thee pain;
But it may yield thee profit, and loss prove a gain,
In the knowledge to cope with the evils that be,
Since launched is thy barque upon life's troubled sea."

He paused, and again on his staff leant his head,
As if he an answer awaited in dread;
With his brow furrowed o'er by the weight of his care,
Like a statue of Patience he sat in his chair.

But soon it appeared he was compassed around,
In the gossamer web of abstraction profound;
And awhile, as he seemed in its maze overcast,
And lost 'mong the ruins and scenes of the Past,

With deference due him, I patiently waited,
And pondered the story that he had narrated—
With the means I possessed of affording relief,
To a way-worn old pilgrim forsaken in grief.

At length the dull silence I ventured to break,
And from his deep reverie bade him awake;
With his means of subsistence, I begged him to tell
How long he had lived in his hut in the dell.

"The brook," he replied, "and the forest around,
With fishes and game in their season abound;
And can be obtained as my taste may incline,
By my guns, and my traps, and the rod, hook and line.

"The fruit of the hickory, walnut and beech,
And that of the vine, are as well within reach;
My saccharine matter—the pure maple sap,
And my clothes are from skins of the beasts I entrap.

"The warblers that flock to the rill are my choir,
And the wavy tree boughs—my oblivious lyre.
So Nature doles out what she will from her store,
And as less would suffice, I ask of her no more.

"But little, my child, do we need here below,
And that may be lessened, as older we grow,
Till the pitcher, as was by Diogenes shown,
We may break, and rely upon Nature alone.

"As appears from my journal, mine old oaken staff,
I have lived in seclusion ten years and a half;
A record was made every night ere I slept,
And as faithful as Time in his rounds, was it kept.

"By a full computation, my years are fourscore,
And soon shall my term of probation be o'er;
In the socket, the taper of life glimmers low,
And little more light will it have to bestow.

"But ere its last flickering ray disappears,
And with it extinguished my sorrows and tears,
Bear witness, ye angels above, while beneath,
A Father his Son, shall his blessing bequeath.

"Startle not! nor thy sympathy vainly bestow,
Though heartily proffered, it oft maddens woe;
Our ills we with patience should better endure,
Than to means unavailing resort for their cure.

"My blessing receive, and I'll bid thee good-night;
May Heaven vouchsafe thee His hallowed light,
To beam on thy pathway and keep thee steadfast
In that faith which will save thee in triumph at last.

"Should we again meet, and the topic renew,
The Past we may feel more composed to review;
But in the event that may save us the task,
Oh! grant me one boon, which is all that I ask:

"When Death of incumbrance, my soul shall relieve,
Fast by, let the earth that incumbrance receive;
That the murmuring rill may the wayfarer tell,
Where rests the recluse of the hut in the dell.

"My secret, I trust, in thy bosom will rest,
Till thy Mother an angel in heaven is blest;
Even truth prematurely, O never disclose!
While silence is virtue, break not its repose."

He ending, reclined on his pallet of straw;
In doubt whether still to remain, or withdraw,
The hound, with the instinctive trait of his kind,
Apparently had my dilemma divined:

His look was so wistful, and piteous his cry,
Dispelled were my scruples, nor could I deny,
Since he taught me my duty, his right to command,
Though he crouched at my feet, after licking my hand.

O'er the pilgrim I leant at the first gleam of morn;
But the burden he through his long journey had borne
Overbore him in age, and beneath it he fell,
And in peace soundly sleeps by the hut in the dell.

EPITAPH.

Here lies the Recluse,
Who rarely a truce
To grief ever found ere he fell:
Asleep in the nook,
That the murmuring brook
Winds around, by the hut in the dell.

    Let Vanity chide him,
    And Folly deride him,
Securely he rests from their scorn;
    Nor asks he the tear,
    Of sympathy here
Denied him when weary and worn.

    In the still twilight gloom,
    Pause at his lone tomb,
Kind stranger, and scan his career,
    But ere thou shalt decry it,
    Compare thine own by it,
And decide as the truth shall appear.

    Thou mayst boast of thine alms,
    Commune, and sing psalms,
And wear a long visage in Lent;
    Attend church as many,
    Without heed to any
Reproof for probation misspent.

    And if by the test,
    It appears he was blest,
With virtues that doth thine excel,
    The Recluse's made known,
    Emulate, who alone
Soundly sleeps by the hut in the dell.

PARAPHRASE ON THE LAST CHAPTER OF ECCLESIASTES.

Remember thy Creator, child,
   While soft and tender is thy heart;
Ere sin shall have thy soul defiled,
   Or youth and innocence depart:
And evil days and years draw nigh,
   When in them thou shalt have no pleasure;
And joys of earth their sweets deny,
   And empty every worldly treasure.

Ere sun and moon refuse their light,
   And keepers of the house in fear
Shall tremble, and the stars of night
   Behind the clouds all disappear:
When low the daughter of music lies,
   And burdensome the grasshopper be,
Or at the bird's voice thou shalt rise
   And flourishes the almond tree.

When fears of what is high prevail,
   And windows darkened hide the view;
The silver cord be loosed, and fail
   Desires, and cease the grinders few:
And strong men bow, and languor feel
   Of age, that doth the end betoken;
Or at the cistern shall the wheel,
   And pitcher at the fount be broken.

Man goeth then to his long home,
  And mourners stroll about the streets;
Or thoughtfully in by-ways roam,
  And solace seek in lone retreats:
Then shall the dust to dust return,
  Restored to God the spirit be ;
And th' living, of the preacher learn,
  All here below is vanity.

DISCONTENT.

Why should we of our cup complain,
  Though it a greater measure,
In the end, shall leave of pain,
  Than it affords of pleasure !

Since we ourselves compound the draught,
  Caprice, or taste to please,
Why should we, after it is quaffed,
  Murmur at chewing the lees !

While we but little joy may taste,
  'Twould equal that of sorrow,
Sometimes, should we less time waste,
  And fewer troubles borrow.

Should we with others justly deal,
   Though ruthlessly they grieve us,
Toward them, still kindly feel,
   When in our grief they leave us,

And in charity abound,
   As Heaven with means shall bless us,
The world, of peace, if in it found,
   Then cannot dispossess us:

The tide of life will gently flow,
   And truth from error shield us,
Earth her dulcet fruits bestow,
   And golden harvests yield us:

We will walk in Wisdom's ways,
   Whose hallowed light will guide us,
Honors crown our lengthened days,
   And woe shall not betide us.

And when from whom our joys were shared,
   Summoned to come away,
We meetly then will be prepared
   The summons to obey.

HADES.

Of Mother Earth I darkling dreamed,
  And hers, by rightful claim,
To her returned, or so it seemed;
  Yet conscious still the same.

'Twas dark, though not too dark the night
  To see, when back I came,
Her face, that by the wan moon's light,
  Had oft appeared the same.

I saw, in Autumn, o'er the glen,
  A sportsman hunting game;
'Twas quail and prairie-chickens, then,
  The season for the same.

And saw him, in the winter cold,
  At a wild deer taking aim,
Whose life and browsing in the wold,
  Then closed by means the same.

I saw the miller tending mill,
  More bent on toll than fame;
And husbandmen their garners fill,
  And drudgers drudge the same.

I saw the pitcher at the well,
    Its windlass, rope and frame,
Whereby its bucket rose and fell;
    And still unchanged the same.

I saw the children at their play,
    And plying her wheel the dame,
Whose infant in the cradle lay:
    Repeated all, the same.

Saw rhymers who were poets deemed,
    I held their poems tame:
If they with fruitful thoughts e'er teemed,
    'Exceptional the same.

I saw learned doctors heal the sick,
    The deaf, the blind, and lame;
And graceless quacks gull's pockets pick,
    The world still wagged the same.

And heard the priest denouncing woe
    To sinners lost to shame,
Who never rise, when sunk so low:
    So live and die the same.

WILLIAM AND RUTH.

"Willie," quoth Ruth, "we're growing old!
   It seems but yesterday,
That we were wed; yet since have rolled
   Full forty years away.

"While twenty-eight but on thee laid
   The stamp of manly mien,
A decade less left me a maid,
   Of enviable eighteen.

"Thy locks that were of ebon hue,
   Are white as driven snow;
And my once auburn tresses, too,
   Are fast becoming so.

"We wearily on the balustrade lean,
   And slow the stairs ascend;
And hence the useful knowledge glean,
   Our journey soon shall end.

"Still, for the last, an easy stage
   Is ours, with health and store,
And grandchildren, the props of age,
   Here gambolling on the floor.

"We bounded up the hill with hope
　　Fulfilled upon its crown;
And will not murmur, that the slope,
　　We must needs grope adown.

"Our path we can look back upon,
　　Without a tear or sigh;
Though clouded ever and anon,
　　It was, that thou and I

"Might trust in Him to make it clear,
　　And learn His time to bide,
Who now and then its wonted cheer
　　For our behoof denied.

"On our wedding-day, a flame was fed
　　With flame, till brightly glowing;
And to its gladdening rays since shed,
　　Our weal is chiefly owing.

"Because of all, first kindled up,
　　And underlies the rest,
The fount of joy's inspiring cup,
　　Whereof we were in quest.

"Still, other fires, thereafter lit,
　　Along our trodden way,
Yet in the retrospect emit,
　　Full many a cheerful ray.

"And one, with radiance streaming far,
  Another scene of mirth
Illumes, where other children are
  Now gambolling round the hearth.

"O, is it then our own to cheer,
  It radiance sheds to-night?
And is the scene repeated here,
  But mirrored by its light?

"'Tis past! my idle dream hath fled,
  Of when as blithe of yore,
Our own, these grandchildren instead,
  Were gambolling on the floor."

And William in his armchair sat,
  While Ruth her story told,
And smoked his pipe, nor troubled that,
  They there were growing old.

Her reminiscences he heard,
  And saw the fire ablaze,
As she the embers gently stirred,
  And felt their fervent rays.

"Thy dreamy musing," answered he,
  " Becalms the ruffled mind,
As often did thy lullaby
  Since when, therein enshrined.

"As fail our lights, by Fancy led,
  In Age's lone decay,
To scenes that life adorned and fled
  We still retrace our way.

"Though here our lights go out, yet then
  As bright as heretofore,
Hereafter they will glow again
  I ween, and evermore.

"But we are not of all bereft
  To sweeten life below:
A little longer yet is left,
  The brightest one to glow.

"Aye, one is left in an employ
  Meet for a tutelar sprite,
And like it here, dispensing joy,
  And radiance to-night.

"And as on opening buds, and blows,
  The summer's sunbeams fall:
It, to fulfil its trust, still glows,
  With genial warmth withal.

"Dear Ruth, this imaged orb of light,
  That rose with radiance jetting,
And glowed in full meridian height,
  Still glorious at its setting,

"Is Woman, in her proper sphere,
  To duty wholly given,—
And unto Man, through his career,
  The highest boon of Heaven."

THE OLD OAK TREE.

Edwin Gray and Jeannie Shields,
  Were children of two neighbors blest:
  With friendship knit while host and guest,
And mutual toilers of their fields.

In helpless innocence, bereft
  Of due maternal tender care,
  These little ones, the charge to bear,
With inapt spouseless sires were left.

Companions in their childhood they,
  Their fathers like, in friendship grew;
  And often in the morning dew,
Their little shoeless foot-prints lay,

Upon a path athwart the fen
  Between their homes, when, o'er the waste
  Their tracks the nursery maidens traced,
To bring the wanderers back again.

But rarely were they curbed so tight,
  As to be baffled in their play,
  Or in their rambles through the day:
Provided they returned at night.

In lapse of time, and when was more
  Indulgence to their humor granted,
  And the matin song was chanted,
They afar, convergent o'er

The beaten track, across the fen,
  And fairies like, were oft apace
  Seen tripping to their trysting place,
An ancient oak, the husbandmen

A landmark left the path beside,
  And mid-way stood, kinglike, alone,
  Upon a wide domain, his own,
Of all within its bounds — the pride.

And there they met to play the morn,
  Until with shoon upon their feet;
  And then upon the rustic seat,
Beside the oak, until was worn

The turf all off its roots, they sat,
  As had the grass been it around,
  When in their gambols o'er the ground,
Their little feet went pit-a-pat.

And once denuded, so 'twas kept,
   As arm in arm they o'er it walked,
   And of the future softly talked,
More serious and circumspect.

Aye there, betimes, full oft they met,
   As in sweet childhood with its truth,
   But in the blithe hey-day of youth,
Without or hindrance, or let

To roam at will in pleasant weather,
   The summer morn; and there at eve,
   Returning, sat to garlands weave,
Of flowers plucked upon the heather.

Ere long their talk had wider scope,
   Though less in sum than heretofore;
   But talking less they thought the more,
More forethought had, and higher hope.

They thought about the path of life,
   They now were entering on, and then,
   About the one across the fen,
In doubt if that would be as rife

As this had been with blithesome mirth;
   And sanguine—thought it would be so,
   Looking for more of weal than woe,
More joy than sorrow on the earth.

The sunny-side the hill and crown,
    They in the fulness of their hope,
    Oft pondered, but forgot the slope
The pilgrim must needs grope adown.

The lessons meanwhile, as they ought
    To be, at every country school,
    With scrupulous punctilious rule,
So by their teacher had been taught.

When, Jeannie to a school more meet,
    Than this at home, now in her teens,
    Was sent abroad, and changed the scenes;
Yet faces met with smiles replete:

She was as kindly greeted there
    As at her rural home she left,
    Ere of its joys she was bereft,
And though she did in others share,

There came no change her feelings o'er,
    While absent, toward Edwin Gray;
    Not e'en when crowned the queen of May,
And meekly all her honors bore,

Was he forgot; but loved as well,
    As when they at the oak had met
    To part, in sooth she knew not yet
Of all her love, how could she tell?

Till strangers 'mong, however kind,
   And the void hours aweary wore,
   As never known to wear before;
He needfully was left behind,

His father's only prop and aid;
   Within his call he should have kept,
   But all due bounds he overleapt,—
To while away the evenings — made

The tavern of a rising Vill,
   A little way below the fen,
   His main resort,— a squalid den
Which with recruitment and the drill,

A fit haunt had become — to lure
   And lead astray a wayward youth,
   Till lost to shame or scorn, or ruth,
Or both, in discontent endure.

When Jeannie had from school returned,
   Though Edwin loved her as before,
   His evil habits, oft foreswore,
He still indulged, whereof she learned.

But still confiding, though distressed
   She felt, till often moved to tears,
   Yet that they were of idle fears,
Fond Hope as often did suggest.

She judging his by her own heart,
    Thought he might not his course pursue,
    Were friendly efforts plied thereto,
And she would fain her share impart.

Still, it involved the questions grave,
    Of risk, and courage rarely known,
    Though even interested shown,
A soul in peril like, to save.

Though many a maiden-blush, unseen,
    Suffused her cheeks, and tears her eyes,
    As Virtue on herself relies,
The monster Vice of frightful mien

Dismayed her not; but under th' oak,
    Resolved she would not fail at need,
    To with the tangled victim plead,
To cast the ruthless tyrant's yoke.

The place and time she fixed and set;
    Edwin tacitly concurred;
    Jeannie had the spot preferred;
She thought he there could not forget:

They were on sacred ground, and where
    They tripped so blithely, gravely walked,
    And of the future hopeful talked,
And built their castles in the air.

They sat them on the rustic seat;
   He, demure, his silence kept,
   She, in whelming sorrow wept,
And both at fault the case to meet.

But Jeannie did, at duty's call,
   Anon her ruffled mind compose;
   That fitly to th' emergence rose,
Till woman's love allayed, withal,

The delicacy the maid endears;
   And gently she to Edwin spake,
   With eloquence that seemed to wake
The echoes of the by-gone years.

It flowed in cadence soft and sweet,
   Untrammeled by the rules of Art,
   Out of th' abundance of the heart,—
That others' to responsive beat,

And that doth oft the hardest melt;
   Fain would we others' burdens share,
   Yet, ignorant of all they bear,
How can we paint the misery felt!

Ah, how can mortal man portray
   The secrets of so deep a well!
   Wherein two several spirits dwell,
In ceaseless conflict for its sway.

The sculptor may his art extend
   To graving outer lines of grief;
   They're but effect — in high relief
Of inner pain the heart doth rend!

And so the orator needs fail,
   Or bard, the fullness to impart,
   Of sorrow in another's heart,—
How well soever he tell the tale.

But Jeannie of hers betrayed enough,
   To blunt the hopes and rouse the fears,
   And soften to repentant tears,
One of a heart of harder stuff:

Whose love divided was between
   His cups and her who knew it well;
   Yet till she on his course did dwell
In melting strains, with graceful mien,

That touch the heart and stir the soul,
   His guilt he fain would have concealed,
   He found to her had been revealed;
When, passively to her control

He yielded him; or feigned to do,
   Without the semblance of reserve,
   Whereby he might from duty swerve,
And for her pardon did he sue.

Nor vainly did he urge his suit;
 Woman wronged is rarely ever
 Ready th' tie of love to sever,
When it shall have taken root.

As fully as he all confessed,
 To deep humiliation driven,
 As freely were the wrongs forgiven,
He had vowed should be redressed.

They parted, but again to meet
 Within her garden bower, where
 They oft of flowers, gathered there,
Wove garlands on its rustic seat:

As when, upon the other left,
 They wove them of the heather bells,
 And daisies from above the dells,
Found blushing in the craggy cleft.

All this to Jeannie recurred, as she
 Was wending home, replete with heed
 Lest she leant on a broken reed,—
If Edwin such turned out to be.

When, suddenly, there from the fen
 A lark arose, and toward th' lea
 It carolled off—an augury,
And heavenly, as taken then.

And promising, did hope afford
  Her acts in woe would her repay
  In joy and weal another day,
Which quiet to her mind restored.

Once more the loving pair appeared,
  With greeting of a fond embrace,
  At th' appointed time, and place
Associations had endeared.

They sat them down in sweet commune,
  Not blithely, as when in their plays
  Of childhood's happy vanished days,
That seemed so short, and fled so soon,

But serious thoughts their minds engrossed,
  Yet divers burdens did reveal;
  Hers concerned their common weal,
His, his own concernment most

To win her at whatever cost;
  His venture grave, put to the test
  While lingered still within his breast
A fitful spark of virtue lost.

Jeannie patient, hopeful still,
  To Edwin's wooing lent her ear;
  His pledges, seemingly sincere,
She trusted he would yet fulfil.

And, since prone to his faults impute
  To recklessness of youth alone,
  And his heart to judge by her own
Now swayed by love, he gained his suit.

But Edwin with his habits fixed,
  Emboldened by his late success,
  The limits of duty did transgress;
Again, clandestinely he mixed

Down at the tavern, long and late,
  In revelry with his compeers,
  Till drowned in sensual pleasure's cheers,
He fell a victim to its bait.

Like many another heedless wight,
  Inveigled there, he there delayed,
  Till in an evil hour betrayed,
Mid the carousal din of night.

Nor was aware till morning broke,
  That by the bait he had been caught
  And wily into ruin brought;
But with the morn to all awoke,

Nor respited an hour to take
  Farewell of Jeannie nor his sire;
  But, at once, in war attire,
His toilet was compelled to make.

And when arrayed, he on the morn
   Was hurried off to Europe's plains,
   Then being strewed with bones and brains,
Of happiness and hope forlorn.

The evil tidings rode apace,
   As are their wont, upon the wind,
   And brought to Jeannie wreck of mind,
In Edwin's ruin and disgrace.

The Channel crossed, and march begun,
   That how should end, or when, or where
   He neither knew, nor did he care,
Nor had a hope the end to shun :

Impending, to decide his fate!
   Or if a hope, 'twas for the boon,
   Of consummation coming soon,
Rather than to linger late.

The hardships of a soldier's life,
   The bivouac, watch and sharp campaign,
   The tug of war and all its train
Of ills sequential ever rife :

And wherewithal remorse combined,
   Though by temptations compassed round,
   With dignity his mien had crowned,
And chastened and improved his mind.

There is no better schooling than
   What is by dear experience taught!
   In Edwin it a change had wrought,
And made of him a better man.

Though on deep troubled waters tossed,
   Without a compass far from shore,
   They moral evils were he bore;
None physical yet — his folly cost.

But graven on a hidden scroll,
   A fearful one events disclosed,
   That in its order was imposed,
And undergone, to try his soul.

The scene was one of mortal strife,—
   And that Marengo, famed in story,
   Where Dessaix immortal glory
Won, but winning cost his life.

Among the wounded and the slain,
   Pierced with a lance and in his gore,
   Poor Edwin lay — as weary wore
The night away — upon the plain.

The ambulances came ere morn,
   But not for him; his wound it seemed
   Hastily had been mortal deemed;
And he was left to die forlorn.

Hence, when the bulletin, that first
   Was heralded, to Jeannie came,
     She 'mong the missing found his name,
And with misgivings feared the worst.

Her wound — nor healing balm nor skill,
   Was equal to; it lay too deep
     To soothe awake, or lull to sleep;
And truce denied to suffering still,

Would not be comforted; and prone
   To dire foreboding — wanting hope:
     She gave imagination scope,
Till reason tottered on its throne.

Still, were remedies applied;
   Still, the patient they imparted
     No relief; and broken-hearted,
Drooping, tranquilly she died.

The herds were winding o'er the lea;
   The funeral rites were duly paid,
     And Jeannie in repose was laid,
Gently under th' old oak tree.

But Edwin with of life a spark,
   And lucid intervals as well,
     Could till Night's sable curtain fell,
The scene and situation mark.

Then came remorse, with restless thought;
   And keener far was felt its smart,
   Than that inflicted by the dart;
From both in sleep reprieve he sought.

But not till wearied nature failed
   Through sheer exhaustion — was it found;
   Still to his vision while so bound,
The frightful scene remained unveiled,

Yet more confused and dimmer grown,
   As paled the moon with clouds o'ercast,
   And blent with others of the Past,
It more and more phantasmal shown.

Thereon he gazed in wild unrest;
   And hence 'twas not unconscious trance,
   But rather incubus; the lance
The weight augmenting on his chest.

While gazing on the scene spell-bound,
   A shadow like an angel he
   Observed, that seemed in quest to be
Of something 'mong the slain around.

The apparition Edwin neared,
   Turned toward him, and by the light
   She bore, that went out beaming bright,
Jeannie unto him appeared.

Excitement consequential broke
  The spell that bound him, when, with fear
  And trembling, in his doom severe,
By dread imbittered, he awoke.

He asked himself, and augered ill:
  "Is this the second-sight? and set
  My load-star that to light me yet
Shed its last ray to charge fulfil?"

But with the morn—an ambulance
  Again appeared, and when arrived,
  'Twas found he had the night survived;
And therefore if the spear perchance

That pierced his chest and there remained
  Could be withdrawn, and he endure
  The loss of blood induced, a cure
Might hopefully be entertained.

The surgeon rendered him the chance;
  Nor vain the operation proved;
  To th' hospital was then removed
The patient on the ambulance.

Full many a year had rolled away,
  Since Edwin home had left behind;
  But through their lapse no missive kind
Had been received; though some delay

Occurred by convalescence slow;
   A message meanwhile as it should,
   Had been withheld, from motive good,
That he the better might the blow

Impending bear; it came anon;
   And coming verified, alas!
   His augury had come to pass;
And with the others undergone,

This bitter woe that crowned his cup,
   Was mixed; whereof full many a draught,
   In lonely weary hours he quaffed,
Till to the lees 'twas drunken up.

With this addition to his grief,
   Now overborne, relapse ensued;
   But Nature bodily ills subdued,
And those of mind for his relief

She left to Time,—but equal to—
   The graver charge of deeper wound;
   Yet this, for even him was found
Too deeply seated to subdue.

Nor was there clearly marked repair
   Of misery in the soldier's heart:
   While that inflicted by the dart
Continued under th' matron's care.

Upon a pallet rude he lay,
  Without a friend, put to the rack:
  With restless thoughts still wandering back,
Awake, asleep, or night or day,

To other scenes; till tempest-tossed
  His shattered barque; its burden mind,
  In whelming billows left behind,
Of hope bereft, to count the cost.

With all his sorrows borne before,
  He now was left, in gloom prolonged,
  To mourn that he had Jeannie wronged,
While living, and her death deplore.

In every scene by fancy drawn,
  Or that in olden memories rose,
  In smiles or tears or deep repose,
She mingled ever and anon.

He saw her coming o'er the fen,
  To meet him at the old oak tree;
  And in the twilight o'er the lea,
He saw her tripping home again.

He saw her in her bower, where,
  At parting, he had left her lone,
  And vowed he would his wrongs atone,
With virtuous deeds and vice forbear.

Again to something lost regain,
   By the waning light she bore,
   The battlefield in wandering o'er,
He saw her searching 'mong the slain.

And with the rest, enrobed in white,
   He saw her traversing the sky,
   Through space ethereal, soaring high,
In endless glowing heavenly light.

But with the lapse of time, as lay,
   The sufferer wrapped in cares his own,
   The war was closed; and many a throne
In fullness lapsed to other's sway.

Though mentally without relief,
   Time having failed him at his need:
   From physical burdens Edwin freed,
He homeward bore his load of grief.

The suppliant of a threefold boon:
   On Jeannie's grave to shed a tear,
   Close an inglorious, vain career,
And that his prayer be granted soon.

The wan moon glimmered o'er the lea,
   As a veteran on an Autumn eve,
   His heart o'erburdened to relieve,
Sat weeping under th' old oak tree.

His knapsack on the bayonet hung
  Of his musket, leant against the oak;
  The mountain nymphs and fen-fowl woke,
As there his plaint the soldier sung.

And thither at the close of day,
  In after time, when it was spent
  In toil resumed with discontent,
He oft repaired to sing his lay.

While many a maid and rustic swain,
  Unheeded by him flocked around,
  To hear the wolds and hills resound,
And moor, that joined in the refrain.

Yet they respectfully forbore
  Approach,—so as to him appear;
  And only nigh enough to hear:
His plaint repeated, nothing more.

When in their May-day sports engrossed,
  He chanced to ramble by the scene,
  He sometimes paused, while on the Queen,
His thoughts seemed to be centered most.

Their joys in others he forgot,
  That lit his visage with a smile,
  And that, perhaps, he shared ere while,
With Jeannie on the hallowed spot.

And when the village curfew tolled
   For vespers, sometimes with the throng
   He mingled, bringing his tithe along,
To pay the shepherd of the fold.

Meanwhile heir of his sire deceased,
   Passively he tilled his soil;
   From his grief and drudging toil,
Biding his time to be released.

It came anon,—the place as meet;
   The harp that oft anights had rung,
   An Autumn morn was found unstrung,
Lying upon the rustic seat.

The moonbeams shimmered on the lea,
   And in the quiet even-tide,
   Was Edwin laid at rest—beside
Jeannie under th' old oak tree.

THE SOLDIER'S PLAINT.

The tribute of a tear,
   With all that to life bound me
On thy tomb I shed,—
   As falling leaves around me:

Murmured in the wind,
   Alike condolence spoken
In soft whispers, when,
   The strongest ties are broken.

Oft in childhood, Jeannie,
   O'er the heath we rambled:
After bells, and up
   The crags, for daisies scrambled.

When in riper years,
   And childhood sports were ended,
On each other soon
   We learned our weal depended:

When we parted first
   Our tears were blent in flowing;
Far from home then, Jeannie,
   Thou to school wert going.

Years, we wore away!
  Thy lessons were recited,
When, our vows of love,
  We in thy bower plighted.

Bright gems like, thine eyes—
  In rims of pearl protected,
Yet a brighter light
  They from their depths reflected.

Graceful in thy mien,
  Deportment unassuming,
And, fresh roses like,
  Thy cheeks were sweetly blooming.

But, all flowers fall!
  And often first the fairest;
Soonest vanished mine,
  Because of all the rarest.

Here, where oft we met,
  I mind, we once did sever:
Since when, Jeannie, here
  We met no more forever.

And, here as the herds
  Were winding homeward lowing,
Thou wert laid at rest:
  Autumnal winds were blowing.

So, to be adjudged,
   At an untimely hour,
Would seem a doom severe,
   For such a lovely flower.

Yet if for mercy spurned,
   Gratuitously tendered,
Then, retributive,
   Perhaps, the justice rendered.

And, if not for aye,
   The sleep profound called death,
But in the lap of Earth,
   Thou shalt recover breath:

Thy worth, I oft have, Jeannie,
   Here extolled in song,
In sweeter strains hereafter,
   Angels will prolong.

MAN WAS NOT MADE TO MOURN.

What though it be our lot to chew
    The cud of discontent:
If made to grace, an avenue
    Of stepping-stone ascent!

What though there be an end to this
    Poor life of toil and care,
Its dreams unrealized of bliss,
    And castles in the air!

As in our childhood oft we chased
    The butterfly with laughter,
So in age we are in haste,
    Some vain chimera after.

Our longing for a void behoof
    That this world cannot fill,
With Nature's evidence is proof,
    Another can, and will:

If this fail, we must strive to cope,
    With all the ills that be,
Relying on her God; our hope,
    For immortality.

O yes, there is a heavenly guest,
    A monitor inborn:
Ever whispering in his breast,
    Man was not made to mourn.

THE WINTRY NIGHT.

WRITTEN AT GENEVA, N. Y., WHILE ATTENDING THE COURSE OF LECTURES OF THE WINTER OF 1841-42.

Ebon Night again resumes her sway!
The moon and stars their glorious ends fulfil,
And as if o'er this Vill, they vigils keep,
Their light dispense on its deserted streets;
The busy clock that strikes the hour of time,
But adds solemnity to solitude.

When closed the toil and hushed the din of day,
And respite given to its wonted cares,
For meditâtion worthy of a mind,
Befitting is the silent deep of Night.

Others round me weary, and like frail,
And in like need thereof, are bound in sleep:
A something so-called when we are awake,
A blessing having, unenjoyed while had:
A cure of Nature for the ills that be,
Or palliative she must needs repeat.

But while material man is bound therein,
A mystery and wonder to himself,
How occupied is his immortal soul?
Still more mysterious, and that never sleeps!
Aye, nor sleeps nor dies! perhaps it may,

And doubtless doth, the boon of rest require;
And hath it too, in some degree and sort,
In sooth, unknown! perchance, unknowable!
Yet limited, while to the body bound
And nor of rest can have fruition, nor
Immunity attain to from its charge.

It watches o'er this tie that binds it here,
And in its lonely watch doth sometimes brood,
O'er scenes long vanished save from Memory's ray,
Our joys and griefs, to lessen or augment:

The sweet and bitter of its mortal cup;
For good and evil done, a meet reward,
Mayhap, and timely for its own behoof.
Or it on high may wing its flight away,
And bask awhile in heavenly heat and light;
And, with its guardian angel, visits pay
Departed souls that have attained to rest,—
Uninterrupted rest! and with it there,
Enjoy a foretaste of unending bliss.

One object only now attracts the sight!
In yonder cottage window gleams a light,
A taper dim, where kindred spirits keep
Their nightly vigils o'er a hapless youth,
Who, having been adjudged to pain and death,
Because his father's heir to an estate,
Or that, in confirmation of his guilt,
He in possession of it had been found,
Is left without redemption to his doom

But interrupted is the still profound!
Some good or evil spirit is abroad,
Whose footsteps draw anear reverberant;
O here he comes, all muffled up in furs,
Nature's auxiliar, subject to her beck;
And who, if in the mysteries of his Art
Shall have been schooled, and wisdom learned of her,
Until sufficient for his fearful trust,
May aid her in her bounteous work of love.

Others, of other callings are but doomed
To battle with their own peculiar ills,
Their share of common, and the incidental;
Thou, with all; thy neighbors and thine own!
To other toilers respite comes betimes;
Never to thee, not even from the quack.

And yet, though lightly oft it be esteemed,
There is no Art more honorable than thine;
Nor one more worthy of its votary;
Nor any votary worthier of his Art
Than thou of thine, if equal to thy trust.
Responsibility appreciate,
Fidelity observe, and keep thy vow.

If so, then on thy mission speed thy way;
At every door may smiling Welcome greet thee,
And, appreciative souls therein,
Be found, above the scum of ignorance,
To recompense thee for thy arduous toil,
With gratitude and commendation due.

Again is broken th' silence deep! but now
By merry sleigh-bells, and the boisterous mirth
Of revelers, who, in wonted haunts have spent,
Well nigh the night, though at a heavy cost,
The cost of sleep, and health, and joys of home
Whither away they speed, inclined to mock
At Sorrow's wail, and still more rueful moans,
When of the precious boon of tears denied.

The tonguey bells, and voice of mirth are hushed;
The sudden storm, that darkened earth and sky,
Whose snowflakes tinkled on the window-panes,
And that the casements decked with wreaths, is spent;
The chanticleers announce the coming day,
And church-bells knell the parting wintry night.

ROCK RIVER.

Or night or day thy shores between,
Of pebbly bluffs, and meadows green,
Or slow and weak, or swift and strong,
Rock River — wind thy way along.

A little ripple now and then,
Thy placid face may ruffle, when
The drifting sand thy course impedes,
Or babbling rills thy current feeds.

As thou from giddy heights dost leap,
And through thy rock-bound channel sweep,
'Twould seem, thou more impatient grew,
The nearer to thy goal thou drew.

And like a fast vainglorious dolt,
Who, loving next himself his colt,
Fain would both Time and Tide outrun,
Were it a feat that could be done.

But when thy raging doth subside,
And thou dost by the rillets glide,
In their soft language thou dost say,
"In one direction lies our way.

"Coevals, we began our race,
Converging into close embrace;
And as united — let us so,
Down to our destination flow.

"The Mississippi is our goal!
And such our fate, beyond control,
We must needs into it descend,
And with its waters meeting — blend.

"So mingled in one living stream,
While sun and moon upon us beam,
May we our course, as 'twas begun,
Then wind our way along till run."

This song, **Rock** River, oft of yore,
Some rambler sung on thy west shore;
And still repeats in many a dream
He has of thee, oblivious stream.

And as he then oft on it wandered,
And as often thee he pondered.
It occurred to him that Art
Would sometime thy sweet waters part.

"And yet if so," concluded he,
"It so forever cannot be.
Once wed for aye, they in one sheet,
To part no more again will meet."

And as he on thy shores of eld,
With thee and Nature converse held,
Still with thy music in her smiles,
The tedium of the hours beguiles.

And while in this wise they are spent,
Still with thee may he be content,
Till his are all worn out below,
To hear thy murmuring waters flow.

And then still wind thy way along,
While generations hither throng,
Thy meadows mow, and make their hay,
And like thy current pass away.

THE VILLAGE BELLE.

'Tis many a year since, come and gone
  I passed a cottage lone;
A black-eyed child tripped o'er the lawn
  Velvety, freshly mown.

Her cheeks resembled rubellite,
  Her ebon ringlets flew
Disheveled o'er her shoulders white,
  And neck of pearly hue.

The rural cot I passed again;
  Less volatile, I ween,
She then appeared to be than when
  I saw her on the green.

Sweet roses culling, in their bed,
  And fitly them combining
With mignonette, to crown her head,
  A wreath she sat entwining.

I learned but little of her more,
  Till years had rolled away
With childhood's idle toys, and o'er
  Its long bright sunny day.

And then beheld, in passing there,
  An angel's parallel;
So beautiful and debonair
  The peerless Village Belle.

Once more I rambled by the Cot;
  When lo, its light had fled!
A dreary waste—the grassy plot,
  And void—the flower-bed.

The Matron lone, that even-tide,
  As if her child awaiting,
A vacant chair leant on—beside
  The ingle ruminating.

"Plague not a Mother, spent with weeping,
  Her sorrow brooding o'er,"
A neighboring rustic, vigil keeping,
  Whispered at the door.

"An easy stage," subjoined the swain,
  "Of a journey yestermorn,
Escorted by a nymphly train,
  Her child away was borne.

"At night upon her bed they strewed
  Full many a fragrant rose
And mignonette, with tears bedewed,
  And left her in repose."

THE TWINKLING STAR.

Serene and tranquil is the night!
   Not even a zephyr blowing,
The new moon sheds her lurid light,
   Mid stars around her glowing;
Ended is the toil of day!
   And toilers all asleep,
Save him who longer would delay,
   And wonted vigil keep.

I see one Star in th' heavens above,
That seems to smile on me in love,
And if indeed it should be so,
So let thy light on me below,
O, twinkling Star, effulgent beam,
As at a loss whereof to dream,
In thee I find a fruitful theme;
And though unlike thee, yet inglorious,
Thee, I'll sing a strain harmonious.

And while I in my rude porch sit,
   With mine oblivious cigar,
Inwreathed with th' redolent smoke of it,
   O may I, glorious twinkling Star,
With thee communion hold to-night!
Out of thy fulness lend me light!

To me reveal, thou sparkling gem,—
If God nor man my theme condemn,—
How many stars in bright array,
Are glowing in the milky-way?
The fixed, and yet not stationary?
Th' wandering, and the planetary?
All, the azure heavens grace
Throughout immensity of space?
And 'mong them all that nightly glow,
How many habitable worlds of woe,
Like unto this one here below?
Wherein his prey the roaring lion
Waylays on the road to Zion?
Whose dwellers fare, as here they do,
And tasks, with discontent pursue!
Like this they all come into crying!
Live for bliss, on Hope relying!
And forlorn, go out of, sighing!
How many are there better than this:
Whose peoples dwell together in bliss,
And, free of every ill, employ
Eternal day in peace and joy?
Like questions, I would not disguise,
Do ever and anon arise
Within the minds of mortals here,
In this dark sublunary sphere.
And who would dare to soar on high,
Had they the wings wherewith to fly,
And even penetrate the sky,
Into its mysteries to pry?

Yes, this is all a mystery!
And unto them shall ever be,
Perhaps, unless unriddled by thee!

O then indulge them with more light!
Not that which charms with sense of sight,
But that which moves the soul and heart
With rapture that it doth impart!
And that will help the weak to climb
Ascents that lead to things sublime!

But lest too soon uncurbed desire
Shall lure them on to reaches higher
Than their strength is equal to,
Because of proneness so to do:
The things that are of high concern,
And that they cannot yet discern,
We'll leave awhile that they may learn
   Some truths which, doubtless, thou canst teach,
   Of things below within their reach,
And then to those above return.

Reveal then now, if not forbidden,
Truths that have full long lain hidden,
From whom it concerns to know,
The dwellers of this orb below,
Who, as it on its axis turns,
Each his own bread and butter earns
In th' sweat of his face, and ills that be
Must needs endure — he cannot flee.

Lend them, O Star! some light, and tell
How long since this—once but a shell
Chaotic—from another fell,
Like mundane, that, as round it whirled
Into its place the nebula hurled,
Which, sphered therein, became a world?
Or otherwise was made, and when?
And also when, by women and men,
Endowed with reaches great and small
Was it then denizened withal?
Though on all these—our quest for light,
To one, 'tis limited to-night.
This problem that strong heads hath racked
The most, and almost weak ones cracked,
Involves a fearful weighty fact;
And might unsolved, perchance, control,
As years away on ages roll,
The fate of many an innocent soul;
And though in abeyance kept full long,
It is the burden of my song:
How long upon its axis here,
Hath this wild world within its sphere,
Uncurbed, been running its career?
This is the sum of all in one!
   The only question put of many,
Decked with rhyme, and rhythm spun
   Having reason in 't if any.

As time is reckoned now in it,
  It has revolved six thousand years,
  Or thereabouts, as it appears
Upon a page of Holy writ.

Yet, this light on th' subject cast,
By lights that burned in the dark Past,
And since hath been upon it shed,
Through ages after they were dead,
By oracles, 'tis boldly said,
Is now, forsooth, forever fled.

Yes—than their fathers farther seeing,
Men have risen now in being,
Who the record hold in doubt;
And that if Moses wrote it out,
He knew not what he was about.
Whether or not he then afforded
An amanuensis who recorded,
Whatso he should dictate, they,
The oracles, have naught to say.
But that this world hath longer stood,
If stand it ever did or could,
Than from the record doth appear,
As we compute time, in it here,
They of all doubt, and error free
Do now pronounce a verity.

Ah yes! aspirants who had aimed
To be for doing wonders famed,

Not by climbing up the steep
Parnassus, to the glory reap,
But by through strata digging deep,
With spade and pickaxe into th' ground,
Aver their aim they in it found.
Whence comes their cry, *eureka!* rising
On the winds of heaven — surprising
Many goodly men of mind,
The sober and inquiring kind,
Who, having souls to save or lose,
And free to good or evil choose,
Their privilege would not abuse.
These are " the salt of earth ! " and who,
In quest of Truth — without ado,
The tenor of their way pursue ;
And when successful do rejoice
To see her, and obey her voice.

But by researches high and low,
So far as their own reaches go,
The wonder styled a verity,
By others, they have failed to see.
And though misgivings not without,
As such they hear it noised about,
They their diurnal tasks pursue,
And wonted rounds of duty do ;
And with self-approbation too.
Yet though so day by day be spent,
And in a way to bring content,

Each at its parting leaves unsolved
The problem that their peace involved !
These in the balance still remain !
And that to solve and this regain
At even-tide in fitting mood,
For this with deep solicitude :
O'er that they smoke their pipes and brood.

These goodly souls in darkness left,
   Since oracles they cannot trust,
Not utterly of hope bereft,
   Upon themselves depend they must ;
On human aid and that, their own,
With faith in God rely alone.

One of them while of light in quest,
   By intuition or a dream,
Or greater reaches than the rest,
   Reports he saw a hopeful gleam.
'Twas when upon his bed he lay,
A little while ere dawned the day.

He had consumed the even-tide
In musing lone, his fire beside ;
And when he had raked up the fire,
And did, to seek repose, retire,
His mind with restless thoughts was still
Replete, and so remained until
Its mortal tenement was bound
In slumber neither sweet, nor sound.

And if the troubled soul relief
Procured, 'twas only respite brief.
For soon its charge — its house of clay
It left, and flitted on its way,
Its airy way in boundless space,
To search for light, it found the place,
By changes made in Nature's face
The subterranean passage made,
Through strata, with the pick and spade.
It wandered down the gloomy steep,
In fitting mood for musing deep,
The layers rummaging as it went,
In earnest, soul-felt good intent.

The visit paid, with what it learned,
It fleetly to its charge returned ;
That stirred thereby, as it would seem,
Abruptly fled the wanderer's dream.

Yet mirrored in his mind that teemed,
With restless thoughts all he had dreamed.
And as upon his bed he lay,
A little while ere dawned the day,
And in the speculum he gazed,
That now before his face was raised,
The gleam, perceived by mental ray,
Grew brighter with the opening day.
And though yet tangled in the maze
Of Nature's darksome trackless ways,

To aid him thread his way thereout,
So oft as, if at all, in doubt,
Now gladdening light the scene pervaded,
That erewhile the darkness shaded,
Penetrating many a cleft,
In rocks, perhaps, by earthquakes reft,
Whereon his foot-prints Time had left,
Which proved he had been there of yore ;
Oft since the flood, perchance, before !
As many an impress — so defaced —
Appeared — it barely could be traced !
Yet though Time on the mirror's face,
His foot-prints left in many a place,
He for the quester left no trace
Of Truth, that others in the well,
Had snuffed and ferreted out — to tell,
E'en with the light that promised aid,
When Time's first foot-prints there were made.
That he to his compeers could show,
And all the rest o' the world might know,
Indubitably, how long ago !

But the devoted quester this,
His promised aim, was doomed to miss!
That reached, would have afforded bliss
To those who prize in age the truth —
They had been taught to love in youth !
And the whole matter, in confusion,
Would have reached a happy conclusion:
An explosion of delusion,

And, tumultuous passions quell'd !
And still in veneration held
The author for his tale of eld !

But all to lose and naught to find,
Of this whole sum of good, combined,
By any vestige left behind
Was happiness to him denied,
Who into Heaven's secrets pried :
Though with as good a motive as ever
Stirred a soul to good endeavor !

Yet though on troubled waters tost,
He found, when left to count the cost,
His labor of love was not all lost.
For while he mused upon his theme,
In heavenly light that 'gan to gleam,
And with the morning brighter grew,
And clearer sheened with the review,
He fancied he had found a clew,—
That him would aid without delay
To thread his labyrinthian way.
Which this new doctrine would refute,
And that "upheld by old repute,"
Restore to whom are heirs thereto,
And peace therewith, that would ensue.

But the report, th' quester laid
  Before his peers with all his pains—
Taken in his visit paid,
  And musings lone and late, contains;
  The sequel only now remains,

The gleam, that sheened with opening day,
  And as it wore the brighter grew,
Till lit the dreamer's mazy way
  The nebular theory brought in view,
  That yet may hap to back him through.

New theories here below abound;
And prove to be or false, or sound;
Or proof be wanting to afford
The theorist merited reward.
Whatso be th' event of this
Bold theory or hypothesis,
Laplace immortalized, none know;
Or if known in the world below,
And secret kept, by any one
For an inscrutable end 'tis done.

But whether this upon the sand,
Was built to fall, or rock to stand?
Our dreamer deemed the last was true;
And gave good reason for it, too.
His thoughts, herein with faith imbued,
He gave free scope—befitting mood:

"Since God made Eve out of a rib,
Who wore an apron and a bib,
As other children do and should,
And grew up unto womanhood:
Why should not He a clod have taken,—
From some mundane planet shaken,
And a ball to thrive and grow
Have moulded to revolve below?

"Was this created so?" quoth he,
In grave and low soliloquy:
" Herein a mystery lies too deep,
Alas! to needful knowledge reap;
Nor hath profane nor Holy writ,
Afforded light to fathom it!
To grope our way in darkness we
Are left till it unriddled be!
Whereof was made this world below?
To farther go—we first must know!
For with the rest—thereon needs turn
The when? and paramount concern!"

Now when this world was made and sphered,
Essential Time needs have appeared!
Then somewhere—there were eyes to see!
And if of any seen, of thee!
Of thee, O glorious twinkling Star!
  Whereof 'twas made? then thou can'st tell,
  And so the tumult in it quell!
Thou must have seen him in his car!

Yet he might not have had one then,
Wherein to ride! for that was when
Crude matter round in chaos lay,
And o'er it ebon Night bore sway!

On sands, and rocks by some means reft,
The foot-prints oft of Time were left!
And, doubtless, many an one of yore!
And many, seemingly, before:
Six thousand years, and they the last,
Had come and vanished in the Past!

"But what, conceding this be true,"
Our dreamer asks, "hath it to do
With the grave question in dispute?
There's nothing of it to refute,
By either party to the suit!
It to the nebular theory that
Must needs be sound, is no less pat:
Than it is unto this of those,
Who for their ends — fain would depose
The author, famed for sacred story,
Of good name, and all his glory.

"And so, the vestiges that bear
Unheard-of marks, antique and rare,
If such were found, in digging th' well,
They were in th' land-slip when it fell

From some old sublunary sphere ;
And having reached its poise, was here
Suspended in the ether clear,
By wondrous power, matter given
To fulfil the will of Heaven."

But while he mused hereon without
Any misgivings, save about
The wanting proof, his heart to cheer,
And render the nebular theory clear,
The hapless dreamer suddenly met
With an impediment that yet
Laplace's theory may upset !
Or if not fatal, troublesome,
At best, be found to overcome.

The barrier, shadowing his way,
And like a mountain on it lay,
Was Holy writ, to his dismay !

In six, or seven days at most,
  He found, referring to his text,
This world was made, and all the host
  Of them, appeared thereto annexed !
  Whereat, he sorely is perplexed.

For some good hap, his time to bide,
In solitude, his fire beside,
A wintry night, prolonged till late,
I left him in his helpless strait.

With singing fain would I prolong
The far-spent night, to end my song!
The moon is sinking in the west!
Exhausted nature calls for rest!
Indulge me, gentle Star, therefor,
That vigor lost it may restore:
And, fittingly, in thy bright light,
I may appear another night!
And if again we chance to meet,
O may it be with joy replete!
The when and where? ah, who can tell!
Yet till we meet again, farewell!

THE SEQUEL OF THE TWINKLING STAR.

As sometimes, on a ramble lone,
A friend I meet, thereto like prone,
As most like solace-seekers are,
With joy I greet thee, twinkling Star!
Ay, greater joy I feel than when
A friend I sometimes meet as then!
'Tis thirty years since fain I met
Thee here, and left thee with regret!

Still, meanwhile, often dreamingly,
 When traversing the prairies wild,
Have I in gazing up at thee
 The tedium of the night beguiled;
 Though never sure thou on me smiled.

But whether fancy had to do
Therewith, or reason led thereto,
Here on my porch content I'll be,
If once more thou wilt smile on me.

The song to thee I partly sung,
About this world, and plaintive rung:
My harp hath lain too long unstrung
To finish here beneath the Sun!
Though it hereafter may be done!

But in th' beginning of my song,
   Where changed the scene sublime on high
To one below, I meant ere long
   To that reopen in the sky;
Yet failed of strength to mount the height,
That charming unforgotten night!

Still, to fulfil a good endeavor
It is better late than never!
And, although of vigor reft,
The little strength remaining left
I'll spend with thee, and not complain
Shall it not have been spent in vain.

Wouldst thou in language known to me
Now speak, O I will hold with thee
More than an earthly colloquy!
As even heavenly it would be!

As long ago, then, from afar
Emit thy radiance, twinkling Star!
That radiance which shall warm the heart,
And intellectual light impart!

And though one childlike may appear
  To questions ask that are too deep
To be resolved by Sage, or Seer,
  Whose life is spent to glory reap
  With knowledge that he cannot keep,

Still, e'en without the glory bright,
Give, O give th' aspirant light!
That light which him—none here can give,
Whereby he might hereafter live!

Since here, till well nigh spent the night,
We converse held in thy clear light,
On th' journey of life I have grown old!
This fire-side saying still is told!
And still without addition done,
Is handed down from sire to son!
And though the problem lies unsolved,
How long has this orb revolved,
Each still pursues his several aim,
Till reached the goal for all the same!
And, as erewhile, the world still wags!
And daisies on the bleaky crags
In Spring-time bloom, and fragrance rare
Exhale and waste upon the air!

Still come the Seasons and depart,
  Alternately, as was design'd!
And joy or sorrow, every heart
  In coming bring or leave behind!

And now, shouldst thou not be engrossed
  With weightier cares, thine own or those
Of others of the starry host,
  Take note of all I shall propose,
And answer render at the close.

When didst thou out of chaos wake?
From whom or what thy glory take?
How light acquire to glorious make?
Whence came thee? and from what thy source?
And who or what directs thy course,
And thee retains therein perforce?

Wast thou created to enhance
Thy Maker's glory? or by chance,
Didst thou far in the ether clear,
An uncreated orb, appear,
Untrammeled in thy sphere to glow
With light thou canst at pleasure throw,
And, on whom thou wilt, bestow?

That this is true, they who believe,
I pity! but whom that receive
As such, I do congratulate,
And honor for their high estate!

Why cast, in cloudless nights, as seems,
On other peers thy silvery beams?
Is it because of inborn meed,
Thy heart is stirred, if one indeed
Thou hast, to others help in need?

Have suns and satellites about
Them moving, each in her own route,
And other luminous bodies through
The heavens, aught with it to do?
In sooth — is th' radiance by thee thrown,
Thine own, or from a source unknown?
Or from the Fountain of all light —
  The all-creating and first cause
  Of Nature, with her wondrous laws?
Whence, while o'er chaos sable Night
Bore sole and undivided sway,
Beamed forth the regent of the day?

If higher power generates
All light, and thence it emanates,
Then that which flows from thee in streams,
Cannot be thine own, as seems!
But thy proportional amount,
Dispensed by that unfailing Fount!

O then the light that on thee glows,
The radiance lends that from thee flows!
And renders sacred every ray
Thou art imparting on thy way!

Thy lotted way through regions bright,
With glorious transcendental light,
Perhaps, because there is no night!

But once more I for needful rest,
Must leave thee in the heavens blest!
My story is, so far as told,
  Without response! though decked with song.
No further colloquy shall I hold
  Here with thee! yet, to all prolong
Hereafter, will I bide my time!
  And, if vouchsafed the boon shall be,
I in some neighboring happy clime,
  The knowledge here denied to me,
  Will bide thine own to learn of thee,

In regions bright, unknown afar:
Till then, farewell — O Twinkling Star!
Thy rounds to traverse in the sky
I leave thee on thy mission high!
Thee, one of a glorious set!
  Even too bright and rich a gem
For an archangel's coronet!
    Befitting, *with all the host of them*,
    The King of heaven's diadem!

THE EXILE.

'Twas twilight when I took my final leave of home;
The sun's last glimmering rays had vanished from its dome.

The twinkling stars, the azure vault of heaven crowned,
And queen of night, shed their soft shimmering light around.

At the weeping-willow I paused, it seemed to for me rue,
As from its drooping branches dripped its pearly dew.

Still oft appears the scene around that ancient tree,
Though now the ocean rolls between my home and me.

The curtain dropt of ebon night, nor space nor time
Can hide it from review, nor make it less sublime.

Whatever be my lot, wherever chance may find me,
Memory takes me back to home I left behind me.

When Fortune frowns or smiles, and grief or joy may bring,
Hope cheers me on my way, or shall have taken wing.

When bound in revery's web, or balmy sleep steals o'er me,
Rapturous scenes of home—sweet home appear before me.

When sheeny Spring returns, with buds and blossoms sweet,
The birds rejoicing sing, and farmers sow their wheat;

When beams the Summer's sun upon the golden fields,
Refreshing showers fall, and Earth her harvest yields;

When gloomy Autumn comes with seared and yellow leaves,
And icicles adorn the rural cottage eaves;

When Winter takes, by storm, possession here below,
And earth in torpor lies, imbedded in the snow;

A scene of home for each, fond Memory still retains,
And light of other days indelibly remains;

And though therefrom reflected in rays perhaps less bright,
Embalmed with olden memories, as grateful is the light.

O ye, then, on whom Fortune freely smiles bestows,
The hapless exile shelter from his ruthless foes!

And if the pittance of truce to care and grief he find
In light that lingers round sweet home he left behind,

Deny him not the sacred boon that, streaming thence,
Reflects upon his way its gladdening radiance.

He may have served his country well in honored sphere,
And for his noble zeal, rewarded doom severe.

Or by some rival, who had loved his country less,
Despoiled of his good name, through plotting and finesse.

Perchance in quest of truth he into error ran;
And though adjudged a traitor, still a loyal man.

THE SEASONS.

Sweet Spring came in with her array
Of tiny buds and flowers gay,
To live her short and busy day
              Of sunny light;
And with the merry month of May
              She took her flight.

Mild Summer came with dew and rain
And fervent heat to ripen grain,
That husbandmen upon the plain
              Might harvests reap;
And Fall left o'er the wide domain
              To vigils keep.

Sad Fall his watch kept, till with care,
Amid the gloom of forests bare,
He looked the picture of despair
              Of joys bereft;
And with a cold and cheerless air,
              His charge he left.

Stern Winter, in his robe of state
And sullen mood and hurried gait,
With howling winds and evenings late,
              Proclaims at last,
As glows the fire within the grate,
              The Fall is past.

With piping voice and stormy din,
And icicles upon his chin,
He warning gives to all within,
    At every door,
That he has come to now begin
    His reign once more.

While seasons come and go in turn,
And through them bread or bays we earn,
A tale they teach of high concern,
    Whereof I sing,
And fain would have my hearers learn:
    Time's on the wing.

Like Spring we bud and blossom here;
Like Summer fruitful, ripe appear;
And like the Autumn, in the sere
    Of age decay;
And like it in the Winter drear
    We pass away.

MORNING DREAM.

Before the sun rose, beaming,
  O'er the mountain blue,
And beamed upon the blooming
  Flowers steeped in dew:

And winding horns were bringing
  Th' reapers to the corn,
Or was the welkin ringing
  With the songs of morn:

I dreamt some one cried roundly,
  As abed I lay:
"O sluggard sleeping soundly,
  'Tis the break of day!

"That thou canst tell the story,
  Rise before the sun
Appears, and in his glory,
  Hath his work begun.

"Enjoy the moments dearest
  This world can bestow,
And happiness come nearest
  Mortal may below.

"The zephyrs vigor lending,
   Weather bidding fair,
And fields of clover sending,
   Fragrance through the air,

"The chanticleers ceased crowing
   As the shades of night
Were vanishing, in growing,
   Sheeny morning light.

"With fruit the trees are teeming,
   So is every vine,
And Nature's face is beaming
   With her smiles benign.

"With glory crowned, resplendent,
   Now the king of day,
His light and heat transcendent
   Deals out on his way.

"The joyful birds are singing
   In the groves his praise:
Or flocking are, and winging
   Their flight to the braes.

"The fairest scene, around thee,
   Shall break forth anear:
The mount whose charms oft bound thee,
   Till the gloaming drear.

"Away then to the mountain,
    Whose mossed rocks are laid,
Projecting o'er the fountain,
    Cooling it with shade.

"There eglantines are blooming;
    There thy bed is made
Of flowers it perfuming,
    As they fall and fade.

"To that sweet scene retire;
    Should peace of mind it bring,
And thee with song inspire,
    The nine may aid thee sing."

I woke! the sun was shining
    O'er the mountain blue;
And flowers were reclining
    With the dripping dew.

Repairing to my bower,
    Meet for theme and time,
Before the breakfast hour,
    My dream was trimmed with rhyme.

HOEING THE GARDEN.

With my hair all disheveled,
    In dust I an hour
Hoed the garden bedeviled
    For want of a shower.

The leaflets lay rumpled
    Or flat round the vine;
And the flowrets, all crumpled,
    Hung prone or supine.

A shower came over,
    But, veering, it fell
On the field of sweet clover
    Dean bought of old Tell.

For a moiety unpaid,
    Tell took back a lien;
Foreclosed it and made
    Wholly destitute Dean.

And long may old Tell,
    In peace with his portion,
On the clover-field dwell
    That he got by extortion!

Should he lose all his pelf,
  Ere the Styx he hath leaped,
May he solace himself,
  He'll in Lethe be steeped!

The rain too, extended
  To young widow Roes,
Who cheated, offended
  And jilted her beaux.

By her maid she belabors
  Proved an alibi,
When the pigs of her neighbors
  She stole from the sty.

Yet while it was raining
  Upon the unjust,
I hoed uncomplaining
  All covered with dust:

Still trusting a rain
  My garden would soak;
Nor did I in vain
  The Fountain invoke.

Now all that my story
  Can need is the "backing"
Of a moral that glory
  May lend it if lacking:

Whom "tempers the wind
　　To the lamb that is shorn,"
The proverb designed
　　For reproof, when we mourn.

In drought, for the shower,
　　In pain, for the balm,
Should we trust in the Power
　　That succors the lamb.

THE REIGN OF TERROR.

EPISODICAL.

In France once Virtue waned and Vice prevailed,
And order to maintain, good men had failed,
And bad men worse had waxed, till fiends become,
To Pity deaf—the dread of christendom.
The guillotine devised to them behead,
Which to the bitter end they plied, till red
With blood of a countless number by it shed;
And when appeared th' imbruted Robespierre,
A fiend of cruelty without a peer,
And in his lair Marat death-warrants signed
And broadcast sent them by his imps combined,

Or seemed to be, with Satan, to torment
The living ere one half their days were spent,
Their Maker had allotted them below,
To heaven gain and, and shun eternal woe.
And when Voltaire, the impious heathen sage,
Taught infidelity to rampant rage,
And being by man's adversary ruled,
The credulous in scepticism schooled,
And weak and vain by sophistry befooled,
Wherewith the havoc more terrific grew.
And when the guillotine had failed to do
The work assigned it, found unequal to;
And other means more sanguinary still
The fiends resorted to, more blood to spill,
For more they thirsted for the void to fill.
And after Vergniaud's lamented fall
Without a hearing the Girondists all,
Too tolerant to longer hold the sway,
Were thrust from power and had passed away,
For all were in that savage manner slain:
The darkest day that was of Terror's reign.

Anon the scene was changed! and what a change!
Among events then passing, passing strange!
Then Charlotte Corday from her rural cot
Came forth and did what fainter hearts dare not.
She struck a blow directed from above,
And to her country's altar brought her love,
A holy sacrifice of ardent flame,
And wrath appeased and earned immortal fame.

And in the fearful struggle, pending long
Between contestants for the right and wrong,
Reason was reënthroned! The storm passed by,
And Peace at last prevailed o'er Anarchy.

When these events were numbered with the past,
And order mainly was restored at last,
To find a Frank preëminently just,
With powers equal to an emergent trust,
That must needs be upon someone imposed;
Upon some one! But whom? to none disclosed,
Though long in quest, to steer the ship of State,
Was then the problem of concernment great,
For in it was involved a Nation's fate,
And that wherewith its seniors had to deal,
And their accounts to render for its weal.

Yet that grave task deliberately weighed,
By reason of its gravity delayed,
Became performed at the appointed time,
And in the end appeared the truth sublime.
Not unto instruments is glory due,
But unto Him who all events foreknew!
Jehovah reigns! And whatso be His will
He hath the means provided to fulfil.
But honor is due to whom have credence given
To fulfil the high behest of heaven!
And whatsoever praise men may bestow
Upon one of their number here below,

Its highest meed on Buonaparte will fall,
And many of them deem it is too small.

*   *   *   *   *   *

So was that wondrous being brought to light
That long in secret slept in ancient night,
Whose name within the book of fate was writ
Ere angel, priest or prophet heard of it.
Before the sun peered o'er the mountain high,
Or dawned the morning in the eastern sky,
His deeds that time hath coupled with renown,
And ere time was, were in it written down;
And till the appointed time to be disclosed,
Uninterrupted through its lapse reposed.

O Fate inscrutable! in vain we look
To learn the secrets of thy hidden book
In origin divine! though of the soul
Disposer, independent of control!
Too high to reach, too intricate to scan,
Too deep to fathom by frail mortal man!
The end man knoweth not, nor can he know
Until it comes and brings its weal or woe.
And that it is from the beginning known
By heaven's high King, and unto Him alone,
And whom alone hath reach to fathom it,
Arose the rock on which poor sinners split.
In sin and ignorance through their career
They grope their way in darkness, doubt and fear,
Without the Light that Truth can render clear.

Yet that pure Light they need and hope may break
Its way through darkness and the truth clear make,
They all are aiming at, or have no aim,
Though few that have, Eureka! can exclaim.

Above their fellows some few wise appear,
But these their bark within a circle steer
Whose broadest limit by a chain is bound,
O'er which they cannot pass, but round and round
Encompassed move, in search of Truth and Light
That only from without come beaming bright.
Ay, here below in darkness would we live,
Nor more respect to good than evil give,
Were they not from another realm supplied
To help us safely o'er life's fitful tide.
These guides gratuitous by Heaven above
Allotted were to man below in love,
And like the end their mission was ordained;
If unsuccessful, he accursed remained.
But should they save the sinner at his need,
Because of Heaven foreknown, He so decreed.
Hence, when so sent in mercy, if rejected,
Or by procrastination be neglected,
Proffered, while undeserved, in love and grace,
And well adapted to the sinner's case,
Responsibility alone, I ween,
He takes upon himself; yet he would screen
His mad career and impious life of sin
Behind these means designed his soul to win,

And claim that if his Maker did provide
Means insufficient, and He knew beside
From the beginning they would fail indeed,—
The soul immortal up to heaven lead:
Means more effectual He should have found,
Or not a culprit hold the sinner bound.
Thus fain, forsooth, would man his Maker blame
For wretchedness of whatsoever name,
Here and hereafter, all because the end
From the beginning He could comprehend.

Such is the fool, who in his heart of stone
Denies that God to man hath justice shown.
If God indeed there is upon His throne;
To any sophistry the sinner frail
Will cleave, to ruin on himself entail;
He holy writ doth search for vain pretext
To sin in this world and to brave the next;
And quoting scripture like a saint, essay
To prove himself as powerless as clay
Within the Potter's hands, to moulded be
According to his purpose and decree;
For honor or dishonor, at His will,
A destiny momentous to fulfil.

Were this gainsaid, why then are those at all
Created who do to perdition fall?
Or if conceded, then there still remains
The wanting showing: God in justice reigns;

As then 'twould seem a legion here below
Were but created for eternal woe.
Such dispensation sinners will revile,
And fail with equity to reconcile.
But should he seriously, indeed, desire
To learn the truth, of whom shall he inquire;
Among the teachers, with, or wanting hire?
In this dilemma, at what church-door knock
For aid to overcome the stumbling-block?

How can poor sinners needful wisdom learn
Of whom nor can it teach, nor it discern?
It would be idle for them light to ask
Of clerics, in the dark, till closed their task
Of reconciling tenets trite with texts,
And with the rest the several creeds of sects.

When they shall have performed that duty grave
Which they needs do to many of you save;
O sinners, be content till then to wait,
For on the pending issue hangs your fate.
Let annotators on their theories dwell,
Though meanwhile you do throng the road to hell.
At such conclusion many do arrive
Who would, if they knew how, for heaven strive.
Ay, many an one would every effort make
To save his soul and all his sins forsake,
Could he make sure of th' way that thither leads,
Obscured from sight by long discordant creeds.

Yet clever priests and deacons wonder why
It is, that in their sins so many die.
'Tis passing strange that *any* fail of heaven,
When unto all so full a choice is given!
But not so liberal is every sect,
For bigotry doth more than one infect;
And more than one the dogma do reject
As heterodoxy, that, since Adam's fall,
His progeny have any choice at all.

That many make no choice, alas! is true;
Abiding events, not knowing what to do,
They live in sin until their days are spent,
O'er th' future brooding in sullen discontent.
But now and then there is, unlike the rest,
A bold, undaunted spirit, self-possessed,
Who on his own resources left to find
His way to heaven, leaves all creeds behind.
And though forsaken, not of hope forlorn:
For in his breast a monitor inborn
Full oft reminds him that he hath a soul
Whose destiny is not without control.
He feels the truth thereof, and that the goal
He sought with others, now must seek alone:
The venture takes prerogative, his own
He exercises with a lawful claim,
And independently pursues his aim:

Threading his way as if he fain would fly
Among the stars in heaven's canopy,
The light of truth to win a prize so high:
His day-dream, winging his airy flight along,
To save his soul: the burden of his song.

But though he traverse th' heavens to reach a sphere,
Among the starry host of radiance clear,
The portal enter of a realm sublime,
Of richer soil and more congenial clime,
For joys he failed to find in this of time:
Too late the coveted light may break the spell
That bound him, beaming from the crystal well,
And in aspiring after, angels fell.

Precarious, then, his tenure shall be found
Of fields wherewith unending joys abound.
The golden harvest he designed to reap,
That tempted him to mount the rugged steep,
Was not for him to gather, but alone
For those who tilled the soil and seed had sown.
And should he eat of fruit he chanced to find,
A bitter taste shall have been left behind.
Like Adam he transgressed, and like him failed
Of promised blessedness to be availed.
He learned enough to keen remorse impart,
And longed for ignorance to heal the smart:
The loss whereof he shall have to regret,
While doomed to knowledge he cannot forget.

Concluded now his visionary flight
In disappointment, that so little light
He had attained, and was so dearly bought,
While him humility it should have taught:
Like many to their aim inadequate,
For wounded pride lays the account to fate.
With aching bones and harrowing cares and fears,
Intensified by cumulative years,
In ebbing life the voyager is left
Forlorn and pitiless, of hope bereft,
Nor compass to direct, nor helm to guide,
To at the mercy drift of wind and tide,
Till by life's ocean wave his barque at last
A wreck upon the beaten beach is cast.

But should some wandering weary pilgrim lone,
Of soul congenial and to sin like prone,
A relic worn and dusty stumble o'er
'Mong crumbling wrecks which strew that bleaky shore,
Whereby the secret from its wrapped repose
He can drag forth and to the world disclose:
O may he, moved to pity, then narrate,
With circumstance the story of his fate;
That though the hapless soul, to ruin driven,
Had been balked, in threading his way to heaven,
A tribute due his memory be given.

VICISSITUDES.

Full of change is th' world below;
   A stage whereon its actors play
Their parts, in drapery of woe,
   Or changeful fashion's trappings gay.

The blossoms of the spring, and those
   Of summer, which their sweets bestow,
And vervain that in autumn blows:
   Alike the seasons come and go.

And like the seasons, day and night,
   Alternately begin and close,
Withal, the toiler giving light,
   And sweet restorative repose.

And, like them all, the years draw near,
   And yet, unlike, they come and leave
At midnight, in the winter drear,
   Ere hushed the mirth of new-year's eve.

Though stern without the winter's rule,
   When gently th' matron sways the hearth:
And hither her darlings come from school,
   There still within is peace and mirth.

Still, at the cheerful fire are they
  Made happy by home's sacred ties;
And there like lambs still skip and play,
  With ruby cheeks and sparkling eyes.

Father, in his corner sitting,
  Tranquilly his meerschaum smoking;
Mother, anenst him calmly knitting:
  Blessings on them all invoking.

And so away the night is wore,
  Till taken th' parting kiss and hug;
And then a change the scene comes o'er:
  Poor puss left purring on the rug.

O, hear the change, now, whoso will!
  That in all happy homes is made,
And leaves a void which nought can fill,
  Save when with resignation weighed:

Many a hall that often rung
  With mirth, its voice is heard no more;
The solemn dirge is in it sung,
  The sable badge hangs on the door.

But still the hall shall mirth resound,
  Though that of others it repeat:
And where fair flowers did abound
  And vanish, others bloom as sweet.

ALL AT HOME.

The fire threw out its fitful glare,
As th' old man sat in his elbow-chair,
Reciting his story, as wont, to relieve
The tedium of a winter eve.

'Twas on a dreary brumal night:
  The northeast wind without was blowing,
The doors and windows all closed tight,
  And th' fires within were brightly glowing:
I sat alone in my easy-chair
  Beside the table, musing o'er
A legend, well contented there
  To profit by the author's lore.
The pendant gas-light 'neath its shade
Fell on my book, which well repaid
Me for the effort therein made
To wisdom learn, as it bestowed
A brighter light than on it glowed;
And while so piped the doleful sound,
The wintry wind the casements round,
I searched for knowledge in a tome,
Amid the comforts of sweet home.

The drawing-room lay next to mine,
With door ajar, of oak-grained pine;
And when without were done the chores,
The dishes washed, and swept the floors,
And all to rights within the doors,

My family in the haunt of mirth
Were gathered round the cheerful hearth;
The mother with her work in hand,
Sat toiling on beside her stand;
The children altogether formed
As fair a group as ever warmed
The hearts of parents, ours were so
With love, and the oblivious flow
Of music's tide, till all aglow.

The piece I do not recollect,
   They first performed that winter eve,
But mind full well its bland effect,
   That gave from worldly care reprieve.
Another, yet another rang,
And then a song they sweetly sang
That in soft cadence died away
And hushed the unforgotten lay:
For slumbering echos left behind,
   Awakened by the tempest beating,
Reëchoing in the winter wind
   Full oft I hear its strains repeating.

Good night! they all had kindly bade,
   And left me musing on the scene
That gradually away did fade
   As *somnus* chanced to intervene.
Still though it from my sight had fled,
Another came anon instead.

With less vividity, and more
Phantasmal, yet resemblance bore
Th' original in art refined,
As if supernal power designed
Its shadow should be left behind.
Wild and weird became the scene,
The actors, specters, groves atween,
Dancing on a moonlit green
That, changing into a melodrama,
Ending in a panorama,
Passed away; when, at its close,
From 'neath the stage upon it rose
With order meet, in pallid light,
A *tableau-vivant* robed in white.

The quiet group appeared to be
Engrossed in something pensively.
It might have been from something said
Behind the scene that to it led,
Directly or by inference,
 Till like a sable cloud it spread
 And wrapt them all in gloom and dread.
Nor passing strange th' coincidence
Of busy and magnetic thought,
Of whom are oft together brought
By kindred tie to mingle tears
Of joy and grief, whose hopes and fears
Are governed by events the same,
And interests that ever claim

A common sympathy, and so
Share in each other's weal and woe.
Or, perchance, the theme that bound
The solemn group in thought profound
Veritably might have occurred
Simply from the chattering heard
Of an old tonguey raven that
Upon a bust of Pallas sat,
Venting her spleen in sullen mood,
Foreboding ill in mutterings crude;
But wherewithal they so were tasked
Proved to be a question asked;
For soon the wall, the rooms between,
That partially veiled the ghostly scene
Transformed became and upward rolled,
As if by magic art controlled;
Whereby I both the query learned
And that the answer me concerned.

And so, from all I saw and heard,
Aware of what their minds had stirred,
I shared in their solicitude;
And that, too, in a sober mood;
Yet not because they worried were
By what their hearts and souls did stir,
But that they all should be employed
In what was wholly vain and void.
A sacred mystery to know,
In heaven above forbid below;

They knowledge sought which found might bring
Its due reward : a mortal sting.
Yet though their folly they might have rued,
Their mystic way they still pursued :
Aye in their minds they still revolved
The question they fain would have solved ;
Examined it in every phase
Subservient to mental rays,
And from an unit having made it
Multiform, in this wise weighed it.

" Which first of all the family group
Shall like the stricken flower droop?
Which golden bowl betrays a token,
It shall be the first one broken?
Which link first the silver cord
Doth bind, be loosened and deplored?
Ah! which shall soonest pass away
Of all who sung and heard the lay?
Which head that every other blesses
First receive the last caresses?
Shall 't be that whose flaxen curls
Are wreathed with flowers, buds and pearls?
Or that with auburn tresses waving
Over an alabaster paving?
Or whose hair the summer suns
From fair transmuted into bronze?
Or that with locks of ebon hue?
Or shall it be one of the two

That many a winter hath survived,
Till, unto frosty age arrived,
In silver draped mock-majesty
It emulates the almond tree?"

The clock the hour of midnight rang:
Awakened by its thrilling clang,
I heard the ticking wheels afar
Of restless Time's approaching car:
Never failing the hour to ring,
Nor delaying to tidings bring
Of perished hope or promised boon,
And good too late or ill too soon,
Resounding ever and anon,
A wintry night in th' aquilon.

ON THE DEATH OF J. C.

I saw her in the cradle lay,
    An infant sweet, in slumber bound,
And, mid the noise of busy day,
    I wondered how she slept so sound.

I saw her when a little girl
    In pantalets,— the child of ease,
Whose flaxen hair, in many a curl,
    Waved in the soft midsummer breeze.

I saw her, too, in riper years,
    With ruby cheeks and laughing eyes,
When childhood slowly disappears,
    And adult age its place supplies.

I saw her like a flower fade
    When come hyemal frosts and snow;
I fain would then the hand have stayed
    About to strike the fatal blow.

I saw the mourners gather round
    Her coffin, obsequies to pay:
She seemed to sleep as sweet and sound
    As when she in her cradle lay.

I saw the grave in silence close
    Around that once unrivaled fair,
When in her long and lone repose
    Her friends and kindred left her there.

I saw them softly move away,
    And marked the bitter tears they shed,
And heard their sighs, that seemed to say:
    Peace to the ashes of the dead.

THE VANISHED YEAR.

To dreamland hath the old year gone,
   And whom he left their fires beside,
May profit reap by musing on
   Events that did themselves betide.

Still restless Time moves on apace
   As if he fain would reach the shore
Of Lethe, that a resting-place
   He may find in it evermore.

With genial light and heat Spring teeming
   Came, and hath performed her part;
And left, as glowing suns came beaming,
   Corn to ripen for the mart.

Mild Summer came with many a blessing,
   Many a welcome visit paid,
And many a home, of want distressing,
   Ere she left it, happy made.

Fall came with frost, that nipped till bare
   The vine that bore the last sweet bloom
On Nature's face, of beauty rare,
   And left her, unadorned, in gloom.

Stern Winter came, and Earth is clad
  In raiment white—an emblem meet
For purity! and looks as sad
  As Death wrapped in his winding-sheet.

Then, whom are by the year departed
  Left, on its events to dwell,
Your tales, or gay, or broken-hearted
  Round your fires each other tell.

And he who, by his own, sits musing
  While an ember fitful glows,
And calls to mind naught self-accusing,
  Sound will then be his repose.

THE INDIAN'S DOOM.

I.

In thrilling notes, the lays prolonged by lyre,
Come ringing from the past, of bards renowned!
With love of country they its sons inspire;
The filial tie each to his own hath bound,
In joy and weal, or grief and woe profound,
When nations rise, loud peals the lyric strain,
And when they fall, with dirges they respond;
In song is chronicled the sharp campaign,
And hills repeat the praises of th' immortal slain.

II.

All Europe hath its bards and minstrelsy,
And gratitude to both all peoples owe:
For songs in honor of whom should honored be;
Columbian bards, who bays have won below,
Their music bring to swell the tidal flow
From the Atlantic to th' Pacific shore;
And others, of other realms, their praise bestow
On whom have earned the meed the wide world o'er,
Till this resounds with that, and asks of it no more.

III.

Yet none have to the Indian honors dealt,
All having him discarded or forgot,
Or may have higher aspirations felt;
Then be the theme mine own and humble lot!
Therewith I am content; I love the spot
Where red men's ghosts like flitting shadows stalk
O'er moon-lit prairies,— where was laid my plot,
As leisurely my jaded steed would walk,
And echoing bluffs at the intrusion seemed to mock.

IV.

When Nature had her wondrous works displayed
In rich profusion on this lovely land,
In sunshine lying, or twilight sylvan shade,
Her children o'er it held supreme command,
By birthright tenure from her bounteous hand:
And with her scenes of wolds and prairies wild,
That silence, adding charm to, rendered grand,
And Heaven upon withal benignly smiled,
Her sons and daughters then primeval time beguiled.

V.

No ermine robes nor gay costume they wore,
Of luxuries unknown they felt no need,
Their wants were limited as was their store;
But He who doth the needy clothe and feed,
Had food and raiment for them all decreed.
The mandate was obeyed; their ample board
And furs evinced His kind paternal heed;
With game abundant were their wigwams stored,
Still sweeter rendered by the zest that hunts afford.

VI.

Of all their sports the merriest was the chase,
When they in peace no enemy had to fear;
They worried then with swift unwearied pace
The buffalo, or antlered elk or deer
That left his lair to 'scape the danger near;
So, after food, with joy they spent the day,
Came home at eve therewith, and found good cheer,
Partook thereof, when night they whiled away,
As on their pallets rude in pleasant dreams they lay.

VII.

The glorious sun then rose and set as bright
As now, when sable clouds it gilds with gold;
The starry host and moon their silvery light
Beamed o'er the landscape new, as now when old,
And cultivated fields their charms unfold;
Then, too, as now, sweet sang the meadow-lark,
And as the white, the red men were as bold,
When arrows whizzed from twanging bow to mark,
And wafted on the tides canoes of birchen bark.

VIII.

They had their feuds, when, in their wonted gear,
With paint on face, polled head the scalp-lock save,
Like fiends they on the war-path did appear;
When foe met foe, each other did they brave,
And hostile tribes nor quarters asked nor gave,
As in the mortal strife they did engage,
And blend the maddening war-whoop with the rave
Of wounded, till exhaustion should assuage,
Or death should end the weakest tribe's relentless rage.

IX.

Yet circumscribed their feuds, and scalps but few,
In dripping gore were flayed off fallen heads;
A summer's gentle rain or morning's dew,
Would wash away the stains of carnage beds;
Some maiden coy, perchance, the hero weds,
She had refused, till valor love did win;
The battle ended, peace its blessings sheds,
The wigwam's wonted cheer resumed within,
The calumet passed round, and friendships new begin.

X.

Those days are past! the red man's steps do tend
Reluctantly now toward th' setting sun;
Forlorn, forsaken, thither doth he wend
His way; though long since had the march begun;
To end but when the span of life is run;
His olden hunting-grounds to foes belong,
Where an honorable name more than one sachem won;
The wigwams empty where the merry throng,
Oft made the welkin ring with festive mirth and song.

XI.

And lo, a ship appeared with a pale-face band,
Bereft of fortune, and their lot deplored,
Yet destiny fulfilled! their chosen land
Became the seat of empire; not by sword,
But pruning-hooks and plowshares had on board;
And like the calm that ushers in the blast,
Our fathers came,— awhile to peace restored,
Nor conscious that the seeds of strife were cast,
Nor that their children would the harvest reap at last.

XII.

Upon the Plymouth rock the Pilgrims stood!
With rapture we look back upon the day,
And wondering at their daring hardihood,
For safety to the Barge, the Mayflower gay,
In dreamy reverie we often pray,
With lingering look upon her snow-white sail,
As on the waves she rides into the bay,
With crew that never did in danger quail,
Though high the billows roll, and loud the tempest's wail.

XIII.

Ay, little thought the godly, peaceful band,
That future time would tell of carnage dire,
When fought their sons with red-men hand to hand;
For peaceful homes to peacefully acquire
Had limited their day-dream and desire;
Nor did they trivial baubles with them bring,
Nor demon rum poor Indian souls to fire,
But rather would have taught them how to sing
The highest praise to Him from whom all blessings spring.

XIV.

Alas! the vending of that means of woe,
Was for the son reserved to blot and stain
The fair name that the sire had earned below;
Which on it shall indelibly remain,
So long as history shall truth contain,
Or sin-bought heritage rich harvests yield,
Throughout the country's fertile wide domain;
And to revenge like wrongs will Indians wield
Their tomahawks while left to fight on battle-field.

XV.

We, our mansions,—they, their wigwams love;
For home is sacred though it homely be;
Dame Nature's child at ease alone can move
'Mid her enchanting pristine scenery;
Therein he only is, or can be, free!
And while we of our little lore may boast,
With what he is and has content is he.
The plough of all things he detests the most;
And fain would sink the ship that brought it to his coast.

XVI.

And his forefathers like he still is rude:
Alike in elements, still unrefined;
With vague traditions is his mind imbued,
And Reason shares his throne with Instinct blind
And Justice: Mercy's seat is theirs behind,
Whereon, and in her absence, in her name
The charming Pocahontas once reclined,
And once, at least, did what should put to shame
Full many a flaunting minx and modish tinted dame.

XVII.

To death was Captain Smith adjudged and doomed:
The Damsel in her arms did him infold,
And with the power that she had assumed,
She to Powhatan cried: "Oh, spare the bold!
Great Chief, I thee implore: thine hand withhold!"
The blow was stayed,—a Father's ire appeased;
His warriors bearing their relentment told,
One right vouchsafed their foes, their hearts had eased,
Though sweet revenge for wrongs might them have better
    pleased.

XVIII.

Then may this instance, one of many, be
Reproval meet to those blest with more light;
That they unprejudiced may pause and see
Their own ignoble deeds, with clearer sight,
Which tarnish fame, that otherwise were bright;
And let the tribute of a tear be shed
Upon the red-man's grave, whose cause was right
As ever Greece embraced or Sparta wed,
For freedom was the cause in which he fought and bled.

XIX.

Philip of Mount Hope, the Sachem brave,
His foes deservedly, perchance, berate;
He doubtless never an enemy forgave;
But not without a cause his bitter hate;
That brought to light, offense should mitigate.
Squando's canoe in malice was upset;
His squaw and papoose left to chance or fate;
Nor could that Chief the awful night forget,
When his dear children's homes his enemies beset.

XX.

More savage deeds of Savage are not told,
Than these of white men, on a truthful page:
Kidnapped were Indians, and in bondage sold,
Mothers and children, with decrepit sage,
Alike fell victims to their brutal rage.
Six hundred wigwams, wrapped in lurid flame,
Were made the sepulchers of every age;
As on the breeze the shrieks of dying came,
With pealing shouts of victory to victor's shame.

XXI.

In Susquehannah's lonely, fertile vale,
New England's "thousand offsprings" came to dwell.
They were a pious band, so reads the tale,
To whom a melancholy fate befell,
And inhumanity's dark records swell:
But here the red-men did the whites assail,
And unrelenting were as fiends of hell;
The war-whoop heard, the glowing cheek turned pale,
And rode upon the air keen sorrow's bitter wail.

XXII.

When pealed the sad alarm,—"they come! they come!"
The parley beat, but swelled the tide of gore;
Full many gentle souls, all stricken dumb,
Now death await, or long in fort deplore
Their confidence betrayed,— nor ask for more
Than life,— a pittance rendered burdensome,
As when all joys the world can give are o'er,
Or dwindle down to Charity's last crumb,
And energy and Hope to dull Despair succumb.

XXIII.

The Mother shared the fate of infant child;
Together they in fond embrace were slain.
The one looked ghastly, while the other smiled;
And when Death rescued them from woe and pain,
The warrior turned away in cold disdain
To wipe his tomahawk and scalping knife,
Or seek fresh victims o'er the dappled plain,
And not while one remained thereon in life,
Did Sachem or his warriors cease the ruthless strife.

XXIV.

The dogs of war let loose from leash to fight,
And blood diffuse, till scented in the air,
It flowed throughout the long and dreary night,
From loving parents and their children fair,
Who cried for mercy, yet in vain their prayer.
O Wyoming! the wonted scene of mirth,
To further sing thy dirge I must forbear;
No more thine offspring gambol round the hearth,
Whose blood was shed until it fertilized the earth.

XXV.

But that foul slaughter must not wholly be
Laid at the Indian's door; for truth demands
A record clear in song or history:
Before his Judge the treacherous Butler stands,
With his confederates, accursed of bands,
To hear meet sentence for the murderer,
If not already in his keeper's hands,
And doomed to pains as pitilessly as were
The victims of the dire Wyoming massacre.

XXVI.

Then may th' unwelcome truth be borne in mind
That though dark deeds were red-men prone to do,
These pale-face renegades, to pity blind,
Were steeped in those of still a darker hue,
And were ringleaders of the heartless crew.
So Nature's children by the blind were led
To ruthlessly their hands in blood imbrue,
Till sated with it from their victims shed,
And dripping trophies from the dying and the dead.

XXVII.

But Thaendanage, the Mohawk Chief,
Whose war-whoop scared the eagle from her nest,
Nor heard that night the fearful cry of grief,
Nor knew thereof, as past events attest:
Far hence he lay in deep, unconscious rest;*
'Twould seem that truth in story pure and bare,
To appetites depraved gives little zest,
But relished well, if fiction in it share,
Though language were at fault to more than it declare.

XXVIII.

So truth dissembled had engendered hate,
And prejudice prevailed o'er charity;
Still on the Indian struggled 'gainst his fate,
Still hunted like an animal was he,
By whom despoiled him of his liberty,
And heritage enjoyed in days of yore;
Whereof with jaundiced eyes they failed to see
To him revenge was sweet, that they forebore
In theory, yet were mostly prone to practice more.

---
*Stone's life of Thaendanage.

XXIX.

Nor from each other, did these Chiefs conceal
This truth in council under th' wonted tree:
"Each as his own, should love his neighbor's weal;
And if they prized the boon of being free,
A common brotherhood they must needs be";
A lesson worthy of a sage to teach,
Devoted to the cause of liberty;
Then was the wampum pledged to heal the breach,
That round the waist of many a warrior brave did reach.

XXX.

But feuds prevailed, and still they disagreed,
Partook of pale-face broils, and dupes were made
By trinkets frivolous, — their lusts to feed,
That they might be more readily betrayed
Into the conflict, — through its gore to wade,
Until a captive remnant they became,
Tost on a westward tide ne'er to be stayed:
Poor wandering exiles, — whom their victors blame
But for their stoic spirits which they could not tame.

XXXI.

And all was lost! for fruitless was the strife,
Save to their mortal foes, whose chief delight
Was rapine, spoil and usurpation rife:
Wherewith incarnate fiends and men of might
The world may awe, but cannot wrong make right;
Remorseless consciences were lulled to sleep,
As time elapsed, till dimmed the mental sight;
Of whom still o'er their children's graves do weep,
And from ill-gotten fields abundant harvests reap.

XXXII.

Their conquerors, I ween, cannot forget,
Who at their ease in luxuries abound,
That they the price of blood had ever set
On their rude homes and common hunting-ground;
But with their foes to cope, too weak were found;
The battle hence, as wont, was to the strong;
And hence the Wrong, with meed unearned were crowned,
And all is changed! ravines and bluffs along:
Which, having tongues, might tell of many a hidden wrong.

XXXIII.

To countless ills is fallen man an heir;
And vain his search, though long it be therefor,
To any find more burdensome to bear
Than that of being driven from his door,
And see it closed to ope for him no more.
The Indian's doom! that in life's waning phase,
And till its fitful fever shall be o'er,
He find no truce to grief, save when he strays,
In reveries and dreams, 'mong scenes of other days.

XXXIV.

So stript of homes, grave Sachems were of yore,
Whom Nature's charms with filial love inspired,
And on her lap drew wisdom from her store,
And in her wilds the envied lore acquired
That even College students have admired,
And wondered that by dull scholastic Art
They only could attain to light desired:
That was implanted in the Indian's heart,
Who at maturity could it a glow impart.

XXXV.

Here all were born, and here were nursed and cherished;
And here they gambolled on the green when young;
And here they flourished, waned and mostly perished:
Where now is hushed the voice of many a tongue
That here, in Nature's prime, with mirth oft rung:
Departed joys! time only can restore,
To those whose restless thoughts they nestle 'mong
Asleep, and whose doom is awake, still more
Severe than was their kin, whose death they still deplore.

XXXVI.

So, children like, we sport with fleeting toys;
So Nations rise, their zenith reach, and fall;
Awhile the world is prodigal of joys:
Nor dangers threaten nor alarms appal;
Anon a fearful change comes over all:
The wicked rule, and when they pass away,
As bad or worse, perhaps, the fates install,
To like them flourish, and to have their day:
And in their turn possession leave to others' sway.

THE STUDENT'S MIDNIGHT MONOLOGUE.

The tonguey bells have pealed their solemn chime,
    And their receding echoes died away;
In silent sombreness, and yet sublime,
    Again within due limits Night holds sway.

Locked in the still repose of balmy sleep,
    Unconscious of it others round me lie;
While I in toil my nightly vigils keep,
    To live in memory — or forgotten die.

Full many an one before me so hath toiled,
    And wasted body to improve the mind,
And many a hard-earned sheet of foolscap spoiled,
    To leave, when summoned hence, a name behind.

But blessed with a cozy study twelve feet square,
    A genial world and of min own creation,
Whatso the event, in mine old elbow-chair
    Still fain would I be left to meditation.

Though of the host that fail the promised goal,
    Still on my dreamy hobby may I ride;
Nor be of hope, nor visions of the soul,
    The fitting solaces of age denied.

Ay, though in dreams delusive life shall ebb,
    From greetings meaningless and coldly spoken,
Secluded in my self-created web
    May I be left in silence, deep, unbroken.

DREAM OF LIFE.

Anight, ere rose a dawning gleam,
Or Phœbus shed a gladdening beam,
An ancient pilgrim dreamed a dream
The journey of human life the theme.

He loitered listlessly to school,
Beheld upon his oaken stool
His old preceptor, bearing rule,
And for the festival of Yule,

"No school tomorrow" heard him say;
The morrow came, and with it play
And jubilee of Christmas-day,
And merrily it passed away.

And Mother tight the curtain closed
Of Anne's crib, where she reposed;
And Father at the ingle prosed,
And Puss upon the heart-rug dozed.

A change came o'er his dream, and he
Upon a hill was eagerly
Pursuing joys, from sorrows free,
And that bring no satiety.

A few he found, but failed to find,
With their attainment, peace of mind,
Though some were deeper in memory shrined,
When fled, than others left behind.

Still, in quest of promised bliss,
Or something near akin to this,
He struggled on, yet doomed to miss
His aim through lure of avarice.

A change again his dream came o'er:
Adown the hill and prating of yore,
With others who like burdens bore,
He groped his way, aweary, wore.

Availed of knowledge, experience teaches
The emptiness of worldly riches
And vanity of earthly wishes,
He turned his thoughts to higher reaches.

His rusty lyre that used to bring
Him solace, he for fame did string;
But loud enough therefor to ring,
His muse refused her aid to sing.

With hoary locks, and deafened ears,
And darkened eyes, and growing fears,
Tottering 'neath the weight of years,
Anear the foot with his compeers,

He woke; and with the dawning light,
Imaged in a mirror bright,
Beheld the pilgrim draped in white,
His dream had bodied forth anight.

JEMMY McFARLING.

Six feet in his stockings was Jemmy McFarling,
Who prudes called a wag, and coquettes deemed a darling.
He might not have come down from high up the tree,
But his head was as sound and his blood flowed as free,
As if he indeed had, as oft he contended,
From Adam and Eve "in a bee-line descended."

One of his chief failings, that none could gainsay,
Was a temper unruly which led him astray;
But the worst of his habits he never disguised,
And which often rendered him somewhat despised,
Was that of imbibing till stupidly drunk,
So lost unto virtue, so low had he sunk.

At first, with his comrades of youth to appear
Their equal in revels, he drank lager beer;
And from which, as its strength by degrees seemed to fail,
To further the end, he recourse had to ale;

But in time the effect of that also was lost,
And the hazard to brave, whatsoever the cost,
Like full many others who reckless become,
He witlessly, blindly resorted to rum.
A potation thereof, that cost only a dime,
At intervals long, he opined was no crime,
And the dubious practice pursued for a time.

But time on the wing, as his dark way he wended:
The proof left behind he his limits transcended;
And, while it lapsed, oftener and more he required
His brain to excite until suitably fired;
Yet the time at last came when, to save his own soul,
Poor Jemmy no longer his thirst could control.

Anight as inebriate he lay in his bed,
Without a sole pillow to hold up his head,
Lulled by the clock's ticking monotonous sound,
A respite from trouble in slumber he found;
But the wind, as it whistled through more than one crack,
Disturbed his repose and he turned on his back:
A posture, unquestioned, for breaking one's rest,
And dreaming, or nightmare, of all others best;
Yet whether he dreaming lay or sleeping sound,
Or was on his back by an incubus bound,
Matters not: lying somehow he heard a voice cry:
"Awake, lazy sluggard, the sun is on high!"

Aroused, in a twinkling he opened his eyes,
'Twas as dark as Erebus, and, to his surprise,

He heard something stirring upon the bedpost
Perhaps some live body, or somebody's ghost!
Whichsoever, or either, it posed him to tell,
But the wind having risen it caught it as well,
As soon it appeared, for it swept o'er his face,
When he grasped it and wrenched it away from its place.

The chanticleer crowing, the day 'gan to dawn,
And his shirt rent in tatters poor Jemmy put on;
And when he his toilet had made, and alas!
A figure so ludicrous cut in the glass,
He alone sat him down on the side of his bed,
With his hands his chin under, to hold up his head,
And in that self-same attitude, till nearly noon,
For the first time did he with himself hold commune.

"Had I gone to bed sober," quoth he, "over night,
I dumfounded should not have been at the sight
That mocked me while gazing in the mirror bright:
There hung in the background of that comic scene,
But a rag of the last shirt I had which was clean;
Moreover, nor should I, myself to adorn,
Have helpless become like a baby, just born,
In the lap of its nurse, with a bandage begirt,
And with the rest wanting a tail to its shirt.
Reform is the best I can do, and I'll do it!
A way straight will take, and then straightway pursue it,
Persistingly, too, if I don't, may I rue it!"

But not long thereafter he haplessly died,
And whether his promise he kept or he lied
Is untold: his comrades — the mourners, contend,
However, the effort his habits to mend
"Must have been the immediate cause of his end."

By its author, grave Critic, to thy will and fate
This light lucubration, of mood born sedate,
Is duly submitted, not for your decision
On merit, lest he be brought into derision,
But as to your making some fitting allusion
To Jemmy, commending his touching conclusion.
Therein lies a moral that, whereso reposed,
Must needs be left ever, or so be disclosed;
Then unearth it, ye powers, that it may avail
The old cronies of Jemmy and others like frail,
And withal for the sake of adorning a tale.

RESTLESS THOUGHTS.

The preachers hold "this world is vain,
   And all a transient show;
And th' more we of our woes complain,
   The more we undergo."
There is much in it vain, no doubt,
And much more than is preached about.

And some of these divines contend,
   " The ills that rich and poor
Inherit and cannot forefend,
   They here must needs endure,"
If man is so forsaken left,
'Twould seem he were of hope bereft.

And sages fortitude advise:
   "If grievous our estate,
And we shall fail to it disguise,
   To not about it prate,
As th' songs we sing of woes our own,
Can solace us afford alone."

If fixed above our lots below,
   Then some are made to mourn!
And all such hapless souls, if so,
   Ought not to have been born!
Or so 'twould seem to finite man,
Whose reach comes short of th' infinite plan.

Though th' journey of life at best is rough,
  If we're foredoomed to make it,
And, with vigor, pride enough
  To manly undertake it,
To smooth it as we may, is still
The best, both up and down the hill.

Then if we well with others deal
  To their appeals give heed;
Congratulate them in their weal,
  And help them in their need:
For our behoof it would be best,
Perhaps, to leave with God the rest.

SWEET CHILDHOOD.

A tribute, sweet Childhood, I long have owed thee,
  I now will discharge, if my Muse aid me sing:
Thou art like a clear streamlet that, down to the Sea,
  Meanders along in the sunshine of Spring.

Thy roseate cheek, or thy bright, sparkling eye,
  So charming while in thine unbroken repose,
Like the calm that is lost in the storm with a sigh,
  On that ruffled Sea will soon draw to a close.

But when with no visitings painfully cumbered,
  Throughout every stage of life's journey below,
Some scene, of which thou art the center, that slumbered,
  Will waken in memory and solace bestow.

Thy grievances still thy kind Mother redresses!
  Thy hobby-horse may have met with a mishap,
And to soothe thee with nursery tales and caresses,
  She fondly again takes thee up in her lap.

In the pond that I swam in and skated all o'er,
  Still enchanting for either, in season, the place,
Thou art mirrored, as on its commemorable shore
  I wander and gaze in its crystalline face.

My kite in the air, or my swing on the tree
  That stood by the cottage where I used to play:
Like a mirage the wayfarers joyously see,
  Appears to me often though far, far away.

And away far behind me I dreamed thou wert left,
  In thy bark in the stream drifting down to the sea!
There to learn that of childhood's joys thou art bereft,
  And that manhood's are not from satiety free.

In the sunshine of Spring, like a clear little stream,
  Sweet Childhood, then down to the troubled Sea wind;
And while it I traverse of thee will I dream,
  Though farther and farther I leave thee behind.

EUGENE WADE.

A FATHER'S LEGEND.

A youth of sixteen years or more,
   In Nature's wilds was wont to stray;
The good old dame he did adore,
   And with her whiled the time away.

Perchance he fled some haunting sprite,
   And thither sped with her to find
Sweet solace through her cheering light;
   Or to his fate become resigned.

His path was on the mountain high,
   Or in the dark sequestered dale,
Where echo often heard his sigh,
   And answered it upon the gale.

Some lonely nook was his retreat,
   Where Melancholy is prone to mope;
A moss-grown rock his wonted seat,
   To vent his grief, and nurse his hope.

Many a swain and maiden fair
   His confidence essayed to gain;
And e'en would have been fain to share
   His burden and assuage his pain.

Naught else was known outside the home
   Of this strange lad, save comeliness
And manly mien; oft seen to roam
   Of all, these traits did all confess.

My humble cot the mansion nigh
   Was situate, where dwelt the youth
Who had become, unconsciously,
   The objective of gentle ruth.

And though his course I often crossed,
   Mine toward the same haven lay;
My bark had long been tempest-tossed
   Before he did his anchor weigh.

I found him on a morning dawn
   Seated under an old elm-tree,
That shades his noble guardian's lawn;
   In pensive mood, as wont, was he.

On my approach he rose and said:
   "Excuse me, sir, if I seem rude;
But wherefore wert thou hither led,
   To trespass on my solitude?"

I answer made the hapless youth:
   "A stranger not to woe, but thee,
I came to thine appease, in sooth,
   And tender thee my sympathy."

He with a struggle to conceal
  Emotion of a nature coy,
Rejoined: "I can not more reveal,
  Than that I am an orphan boy.

"Then urge me not, in charity,
  My secrets further to disclose;
'Twould pain inflict on both, for me
  To drag them out from their repose.

"The crosses mortals have to bear,
  'Twere cowardice to try to shun;
Would we a crown in heaven wear,
  Unaided should the prize be won."

Wherewith he bowed, and went his way
  In wonted loneliness to roam;
And thus dismissed summarily,
  I hence anon betook me home.

But moved by zeal importunate,
  With love and pity in accord,
Or the resistless power of fate,
  I o'er him kept both watch and ward.

A summer's night, when homeward bound,
  Aweary by a visit long,
I heard his voice afar resound,
  Though not the burden of his song.

With anxious care and cautious tread
  I turned me toward his retreat,
Where he at early dawn had sped,
  To seek in Nature solace sweet.

High o'er a cascade's fearful tide,
  Whence stoughter hearts might well recoil,
I on a mossy rock espied
  The object of my thankless toil.

The stars and waning moon their light
  Shed down upon the scene, as if,
In high relief, to like a sprite
  Portray him—standing on the cliff.

Stirred not by vain pretentious show
  Of friendship, but unfeigned concern,
I could not, though by stealth, forego
  My hap, more of the youth to learn.

Up its shaded, cragged side
  I crept, till unto him anear;
That whatsoever should betide,
  I might the better see and hear.

As was the covert nook attained,
  He sat him down upon the stone,
And long in silence deep remained,
  Engrossed in meditation lone.

But from th' oblivious scene around,
   That stirred ennobling thoughts, he woke,
And rising, with a bow profound,
   Uncovered, thus the silence broke:

"Whose hand, with awe I ask, whose hand
   Hath done this work? Power divine
Seems stamped thereon, and none so grand,
   Could have appeared without design.

"Above the spiral moss-capped Mount,
   Beneath, and in the moonbeams pale,
Shimmering from its crystal fount,
   The streamlet winding down the vale.

"And hanging o'er the limpid stream,
   And mirrored in it, charming flowers;
O, that I might away life dream,
   In this the fairest of Nature's bowers!

"How wondrous and sublime the view!
   A night-scene with its shade and light
Inimitable! and pearly dew,
   Like moon-lit jewels sparkling bright.

"God's noblest work, 'tis said, was man;
   Then fallen far hath he, I ween,
Who would, while under fearful ban,
   Ascribe to chance so grand a scene.

"From such I unto Nature flee,
 And solace find in calm retreat."
Wherewith, his quaint soliloquy
 Concluded, he resumed his seat.

To serve him I impatient grew,
 And, risking his repulse again,
Intrepidly I toward him drew,
 Desired knowledge to attain.

And thus I spoke: "Poor child of grief,
 Though hither I come, intrusively,
If mortal may bring thee relief,
 Its instrument I fain would be.

"The ills of life I long have borne,
 And well can feel another's woe;
Afar in thine I heard thee mourn,
 And hither came to pity show.

"What fortune hath, I thee entreat,
 Embittered so thy morn of life?
As man the ills that be shall meet,
 More equal then becomes the strife.

"Nor longer, then, from me withhold
 Thy confidence, and shall be made
This priceless gem, enshrined in gold,
 The forfeiture of trust betrayed."

He eagerly the jewel clutched,
    As if through blended hope and fear;
And as its spring he gently touched,
    A lady's image did appear.

"No pledge is wanting," answered he,
    As it he to his bosom bore,
"Thy debtor I indeed shall be,
    Should peace it unto me restore.

"A friendly tender why contemn,
    That light and knowledge may bestow?
Should I reject a sparkling gem,
    That on my way a ray may throw!

"Ay, it may prove a key, at last,
    The mystery to penetrate,
That like a cloud hath overcast
    My path, and rendered desolate."

As on his theme that promised weal
    Involved he anxiously did dwell,
Adown his cheeks the tears did steal,
    Like dew that from the flowers fell.

"In Hope trust not," I answered, "who
    Is prone to lead her dupes astray;
Though sometimes to them she is true,
    As, oft proves false, to their dismay.

"With promise fair, in grief, of joy,
 And lavish of her smiles in danger,
I know full well, unhappy boy,
 For to her freaks I am no stranger.

" That ring, which seems to thee remind
 Of cares in life eventful thine,
Involves those of another kind,
 And such as appertain to mine.

"I it some eighteen weary years
 Have as a sacred souvenir kept ;
Through hope deferred and anxious fears,
 Have cherished it and o'er it wept.

" As such, a pledge of faith 'twas made,
 Redeemable another day ;
But O, how dearly have I paid
 For trust in Hope's benignant sway.

" No longer then on her rely ;
 Like a spoilt child thou shalt her find,
That, when abroad, will patience try,
 Yet cannot well be left behind.

"Thy secret unto me disclose ;
 Thy story known to thee, reveal ;
All safely shall with me repose,
 That truth and honor may conceal."

"But little, sir," was his return,
  " Have I to tell, but will concede
Your right that little now to learn;
  Then hear and use it with due heed.

"The master of yon mansion, he
  In whom I have a father found,
Says my mother died at sea,
  While to this land of freedom bound.

"On the same steamer of the line
  That traversed it, he with her met;
But who she was — save mother mine —
  No sign she gave, discovered yet.

"She gave me birth and passed away,
  But not until her friends and foes
She had bequeathed a legacy:
  Pardon to these and love to those.

"For one who wore a certain ring
  Her prayers to heaven did oft ascend;
From whom our joys can only spring,
  Or solace that can grief forefend.

"Her likeness she intrusted to
  My guardian, as she on him smiled;
'Take it, kind sir,' she said, 'and you
  Thereby may benefit my child.

" 'A counterpart thereof, if saved,
   Contained within a diamond ring,
Worn by a friend, hath on it graved
   My name, discovered by a spring.

" 'My story he will truly tell,
   If with the token found he be,
And as he shall upon it dwell,
   My child will bless my memory.'

"She fell asleep, and in it fled
   A mother's spirit whelmed in woe,
That to a fount its way did thread,
   Whence troubled waters never flow.

"The corse embalmed in spices sweet,
   Within her state-room honored lay,
Till dust its kindred dust did meet,
   Where it was left to lone decay.

"A cleft in this tall cliff the place;
   Whose crown, my rural seat, moss-grown,
Bears this inscription on its face,
   That may be traced: TO THE UNKNOWN.

" My guardian took me home and bade
   Me ready welcome to its fare;
And there they call me Eugene Wade,
   And treat me with fraternal care.

"Yet would I rather in the earth,
    Here with my Mother be at rest,
Than live in Ignorance of birth,
    With dread tumultuous in my breast.

"My simple narrative is told,
    And should this prove the long lost ring,
That brought to light would all unfold,
    It joy and peace will to me bring."

While he supplied events so strange,
    I fell like one in nightmare's fangs,
Whose grip doth motor nerves derange,
    As on its victim's chest it hangs.

It was a bitter mixed with sweet,
    A compound cup of joy and woe;
Perhaps a retribution meet,
    For good and evil done below.

Alas! extinct, hope's dark'ning light,
    That oft dispensed a fitful ray;
Yet shall I not alone at night,
    Be left to watch for dawning day.

For Heaven hath led me, in His ways
    Inscrutable, to find a son;
With joyful tears I'll sing His praise,
    Though blent with sorrowful, they run.

A parent's part He volunteers,
  And well the service doth fulfil;
Though sometimes hard our lot appears,
  The end, submission to His will.

The while I thus soliloquized,
  As wont in lonely vigils kept,
My child his status realized,
  And in my arms with joy he wept.

"The missing link it needs," said I,
  "To render whole the chain of events,
And close the scene, though with a sigh,
  That life so dark a phase presents.

"As in sweet childhood's plays, alone,
  Youth's sunny hours we passed away;
Till age and love mature had grown,
  With even pace from day to day.

"Thy Mother ranked too high by birth,
  As claimed her sire, to with me mate;
Though high and low reach in the earth,
  One common level soon or late.

"And all appeals to him — his heart —
  Moved not, though made with sighs and tears;
No pity had he to impart,
  And deaf to sorrow's cry, his ears.

"Yet the patrician's jaundiced sight,
   Our ardor only did provoke;
And whether in the wrong or right,
   Than his — we chose a lighter yoke.

"The yoke of marriage covenant;
   Which had, it seems, upon us lain
Till death! Ere long our way we bent,
   To seek our fortune o'er the main.

"But heralded anon, our flight,
   And thwarted fatally, our scheme;
Our passports were revoked, and night
   Like gloom eclipsed our morning dream.

"'In free Columbia trust to meet,
   Thine ever faithful wife,' said she,
"'Whose heart, though rent, will meanwhile beat,
   My husband, dear, alone for thee.'

"The fond and last embrace prolonged
   With sighs and sobs, and wild lament
Of hapless consorts, cruelly wronged,
   Together were in parting blent.

"In sailor guise I hither fled,
   And long in hope deferred have waited
Her coming — but to find her dead,
   And virtuous love severely fated.

"Ah, 'tis a bitter cup! and yet
    It might have more of rue contained!
Then I should not the fact forget,
    Less sweet therein would have remained.

"Then let us wend our way resigned,
    As fitting to our cottage rude;
And in the tie of kindred find
    A balm to sweeten solitude.

"For nature's wants, rich fields, mine own,
    Yield ample fruits, nor will the boon
Of entrance to this seat moss-grown,
    Our friend deny us for commune.

"But no! my child, in all our woe,
    I mind he was indeed our friend!
Whom more than we can pay we owe;
    Too much to heedlessly offend.

"All thou hast learned to him convey,
    And add his counsel, in our strait,
And will control our destiny;
    And that his pleasure we await.

"We know the goodness of his heart,
    And so its dictates will abide;
The morning dawns! and we must part,
    But here to meet at eventide."

And at the trysting-place we met;
  "Dear father," said my darling boy,
"My guardian, as we call him yet,
  Thy message hath received with joy.

"Joy that with smiles his visage lit;
  But thoughts long slumb'ring in his brain
Were roused, and soon his brows were knit
  As if thy story gave him pain.

"When thy desire of ingress here
  I touched upon, he bade me say:
The cliff that is to thee so dear,
  And grounds that reach to the highway,

"In all directions it around,
  And also of encumbrance free,
As on the record may be found,
  Were long ago conveyed to me.

"He also bade me thee invite
  To call on him without delay;
And if convenient e'en to-night;
  His coach to thither thee convey,

"Now standing at the eastern gate,
  And groom with steed to lead, and thine
Drive home, as well thy pleasure wait.
  Yet, ere we leave this sacred shrine,

"While much of others thou hast told,
  But little of thyself is heard;
Fain would I have thee more unfold,
  Of what could only be inferred.

"Of thine affairs I this have learned:
  In Medicine thou hast been schooled,
And in its practice have discerned
  Art by its ethics strictly ruled.

"Yet that which on this hallowed spot
  I trusted thou wouldst render clear,
Like all the rest, thou hast forgot,
  Or would have made it so appear:

"As doctor Wade thou art addressed,
  And as doctor Gregg as well;
This myst'ry, it must be confessed,
  How to unriddle I cannot tell."

"My child," I answered, "that upon
  I ought to have more fully dwelt;
But too much pain have undergone,
  For sympathy due to thee have felt.

"To both the names, though little more
  Than them, I was my father's heir;
And on my voyage this I bore,
  And that left with my wife to bear.

"And with it left a parting tear,
   And means, that should she cross the main
Unhurt, her way would render clear
   My whereabouts to ascertain.

"With him who tills my fields, his wife
   Who serves my meals, I served at sea,
Throughout a course of fever, rife;
   Hence old acquaintances are we.

"And hence, the name they knew me by
   In traversing the sea when ill,
And helped to weave a silken tie,
   Grown firm with time, they know me still.

"Aught else of th' Past, I trust, now may
   For claim more urgent be deferred:
Our future pending, we needs weigh,
   Wherein our friend is to be heard.

"His invitation, tell him I
   Accept as frankly as it was given;
But rest my powers need, well nigh
   To helpless enervation driven.

"We'll now, my son, with caution thread
   Our way adown the dizzy height,
Each to his own but softer bed
   Than he hath found for many a night."

"Permit me, father," he returned,
"A word in parting due to thee:
Enough I at her tomb have learned,
To bless my mother's memory."

THE LIGHT OF THE PAST.

The old year drawing to a close,
Pensive Memory from repose
   Required, awakes;
And to the scenes left in the Past,
Wheresoever its light is cast,
Her visits, faithful to the last,
   She yearly makes.

A glimmer, shimmering on her way,
Is like the setting sun's last ray,
   O'erlaying the tomb;
It lingers on the everglades,
And valleys hid in mountain shades,
Sequestered, calm retreats pervades,
   And gilds the gloom.

When sleigh-bells ring with music sweet,
They many a thrilling tale repeat
   We can't forget,
Of other bells a winter's night,
And other eyes all sparkling bright,
Of other days whose hallowed light
   Is lingering yet.

Then, on thy gossamer pinions fly,
Fond Memory, back to days gone by,
   Lain hid in night;
And there on ruins muse, in seeming
Phantoms rising as in dreaming,
Or like tableaux in the gleaming
   Of soft twilight.

To haunts of peace return once more,
But such as cannot it restore,
   O, enter not!
We'll cull the sweets we may of those,
But these that have none to disclose,
Will leave in undisturbed repose,
   To be forgot.

There will we muse in that soft light,
There while away the hours of night
   That reigns profound;

And dream of other bells that rung,
And hearts that throbbed with ours when young,
And now are mouldering unstrung,
   Low in the ground.

And though in palsied life's decline,
Of joy the Present gives no sign
   When most in need;
Its lights all vanishing away,
Darkening with our own decay,
Still, the Past will lend a ray,
   As earned the meed.

Ay, when all others have gone out,
'Twill linger olden scenes about,
   The void to fill;
And, than the glory of the Moon
When at her full, or Sun at noon
Will be, as age decays, a boon
   More glorious still.

And then, though sorrows shall abound,
And friends depart that sat around
   Our New-Year's fires;
The Past will still its light bestow,
And, taper-like, in waning low,
Emit a ray of dazzling glow,
   As it expires.

INGLE-SIDE.

Sweet home in the evening, with those we love dearest,
    Its bright ingle snugly all gathered around,
Is where we to heaven may oft approach nearest,
    While to the frail body the spirit is bound.

Though seekers of pleasure roam whithersoever,
    Its bait they are lured by till even supplied
To satiety, still, they are recompensed never
    For comfort foregone at sweet home's ingle-side.

When closed is the day, and the evening meal
    Partaken of heartily, often with pride
The virtuous household as heartily feel
    There is no place for comfort like home's ingle-side.

And among all who roam far abroad it to find,
    And on railways, and seas rough or smooth, speed and
        glide,
There is now and then one finds he left it behind;
    And it only is found at sweet home's ingle-side.

Where fools by the siren are lured and delighted
    With orgies which none but the worthless can bide;
The parents revered, with their children united
    In love, are assembled round home's ingle-side.

While Vice stalks abroad in his manifold guises,
    And night lends its curtain his traces to hide,
In her sphere gentle Virtue, its queen, exercises
    Her sway, joy-inspiring, at home's ingle-side.

When the winter's cold blast in the evening is howling,
    And the god of the storm on the whirlwind doth ride,
All moonless and starless, the heavens are scowling,
    There is no place so grateful as home's ingle-side.

Would we pause on the slope of life's hill in descending,
    Look back, and feel with our career satisfied,
And look forward in peace as our journey is ending,
    All must needs be well at sweet home's ingle-side.

Were life but a dream, and without any token
    Of worldly care ceasing, still at eventide,
When rest is thereby the least apt to be broken,
    The dream would be sweetest at home's ingle-side.

O then, to this centre of life, or its dreaming,
    May the light in the window at eve be my guide;
Withal, may I meet with the smiles ever beaming
    Of welcome and love at sweet home's ingle-side.

THE WATCHER'S RAMBLE.

O come with me, mine old, tried friend!
   Poor wearied nature needs relief;
In th' morning air our way we'll wend,
   And seek from care a respite brief.

Put out the waning taper's glow;
   With night our lonely vigils close;
To sleep the patient seemed to go,
   Freed from all ills his long repose.

Full many a wistful look he cast
   The window toward for the dawn;
That breaking in the east at last,
   The face of death it gleamed upon.

Our part is done! the sacred trust!
   To others' charge we leave the rest:
The body to return to dust,
   And soul to be or lost or blest.

Then o'er the moor let us away
   To Nature's wilds with charms replete,
And 'mong her peaceful scenes delay
   Till comforted in our retreat.

Our pathway though by thorns encumbered,
  It is shaded by the yew,
And is with flowers lined unnumbered,
  Dripping in the morning dew.

And as the sunbeams on them play,
  And dewdrops sip, that weigh them down,
They seem to greet the god of day
  With sparkling jewels for his crown.

We pass the cascade's foamy sheet,
  And watch below the eddies boil;
And pause where glides beneath our feet
  The streamlet resting from its toil.

Like diamonds in whose sunlit bed
  Lie pearly pebbles dazzling bright;
'Tis here the lowing herds, full fed,
  While winding homeward, drink at night.

And now we rise where verdant pines
  In zephyrs soft waft to and fro,
As on the cliff above us shines
  And melts the last of winter's snow.

And here, at length, the nook is found!
  The calm retreat from worldly care;
With Nature's moss-grown, rocky mound,
  Prepared at need for us to share.

As merrily the warblers sing,
   They seem to give us kindly greeting,
Make with joy the welkin ring,
   And all are happy at the meeting,

O let us here an hour employ
   In looking o'er the way we wended :
Rough and smooth, in grief and joy,
   Which were as wont together blended.

If good appeared in greater measure
   Than of evil to abound,
It was because, in quest of pleasure,
   Heedfully we chose our ground.

Throughout our day, then, as begun,
   May Wisdom guide us by her light
To seek the sweet, and bitter shun,
   That we may rest in peace at night.

CRITIQUE OF BYRON'S ODE TO NAPOLEON.

I.

"'Tis done!" and thou hast done a wrong,
    Both to the bard and king,
Like mortal, in so wild a song,
    About "so mean a thing,"
As that "miscalled the Morning Star,
Nor man nor fiend has fallen so far!"
    Tirade no charm can bring,
Not e'en with rhythmic ray; a Pitt
In prose could only warrant it!

II.

"A Homicide! ill minded man!
    Dark Spirit!" railing keen,
The woof and warp of a metrical ban
    A despot's shame to screen,
Or bolster a waning nation's pride;
Or jealousy, mayhap, did guide
    Thy pen to vent thy spleen,
When that Star appeared on high,
Eclipsing others in the sky.

III.

'Tis strange that men with honors crowned,
    Descend to 'throwing stones,'
Which may in hitting th' mark rebound
    And break the assailant's bones;
But when unbridled passions rule,
The wisest sometimes play the fool.
    Then with her harshest tones,
In Byron's mood, how could his Muse,
Though wild his theme, her aid refuse!

IV.

'Tis trifling with a well-earned name,
    And envied, noble Bard,
To heedlessly thy peer defame,
    And th' sequel disregard!
I would not, dare not treat thee ill!
While wrong herein, I love thee still,
    Thy works still more, though marred;
A blessing on the world bestowed,
I ween, by an offensive ode.

V.

The man who wept o'er battles won,
   Shed not a tear when lost,
Abhorred fell war he could not shun,
   When counting o'er the cost;
Held out the flag of truce to foes,
   And longed for permanent repose,
While in life's tempest tossed;
Could not a "thing" so graceless be,
As to deserve thine obloquy.

VI.

In Hohenlinden's battle-field,
   When hushed the cannon's roar,
To soothe them, by the dying kneeled,
   Left in their dribbling gore;
And pondering the dappled snow,
Discerned the blood that yet must flow,
   And he must yet deplore,
As oft to have the carnage cease
He sued, but sued in vain for peace.

VII.

When at Marengo fell Dessaix,
   In turning the battle's tide,
Forlorn of hope to win the day,
   And knelt his corse beside;
How felt "fair freedom's mightiest foe,"
While balmy tears to weep his woe
   Were at the fount denied?
The battle won, more than if lost
He mourned, because a friend it cost.

VIII.

Whene'er stern Justice called aloud
   The culprit to his bar,
A suppliant he for mercy bowed,
   Whose lustre beamed afar;
But to thine envious, jaundiced eye,
Hidden did the glory lie
   Of that clear "Morning Star!"
Yet, in Fame's constellation bright,
'Twill evermore emit its light!

IX.

Who, then, caused the widow's wail?
   Who shed the gore Earth drank,
Till many a barren hill and dale
   Teemed with verdure rank?
Are Austria and proud Albion free
Of all accountability?
   And must the scapegoat Frank
Bear all the sins his foes committed,
And Satan by them be outwitted?

X.

Nor of that iron war the cause,
   Nor of its sorrows he!
Abuse of international laws
   And arrogance at sea,
Have fertilized with blood and brains
From all the world all Europe's plains,
   To foster Tyranny!
O, thou immortal Fox, reveal
The truth his foes fain would conceal!

XI.

His idol, France! His aim of life
   An heir to crown her glory,
And a name, when ceased the strife,
   Leave to adorn her story!
Hence th' divorce his foes called wrong,
And that in song thou dost prolong!
   Still, therefor, when hoary,
Solely he the cud of rue
In solitude was doomed to chew.

XII.

The bard who should uphold the act,
   Proved worthy of the name,
And due reward have reaped, in fact,
   The world might hold to blame;
Some hold the sacred tie to sever
Unpardonable, by whomsoever,
   Though a shrew to tame;
Yet felons, as court records show,
Unshackled and unpunished go.

XIII.

He on his country's altar laid
   The bleeding lamb, his mate,
And rarely hath mere mortal made
   A sacrifice so great;
He her no less than theretofore
Did love, but loved his country more,
   And yielded to his fate;
'Twas but an error in his creed,
He leant upon a broken reed.

XIV.

Were it alone to glut with strife
   His thirst for fame, indeed,
That led him to divorce his wife,
   And cause her heart to bleed;
Had he profaned the nuptial bed,
And fallen so low as vice to wed,
   The world might then concede:
"From punishment was never screened
Nor fallen so far nor man nor fiend!"

XV.

O, hate and envy leave to prose
   And history profane!
What Muse could lure thee with her gloze
   To sing so harsh a strain!
In nobler sentiments indulge,
Act well thy part! the truth divulge
   And sacredly maintain!
Have charity for fallen man,
And leniently his actions scan.

XVI.

There is no boon the world bestows,
   With or without delay,
Like a good name, that while it goes
   It cannot take away;
He earned his laurels! thou thy bays!
The meed of each immortal praise,
   Adjudged by whom bore sway,
And who no more to you can dole,
Save each a share in a common goal.

THE MIRROR OF LIFE.

'Tis fitting man should sometimes gaze
In th' mirror of life, and, through the maze,
The wildering maze of vanished years,
Retrace his steps in smiles or tears.

If he in doubt his way shall grope,
Nor ray of light, nor faith, nor hope
Can in the retrospection find,
It only leaves a sting behind.

But if he can without remorse
Or fear look back upon his course,
Some lingering ray will comfort bring,
And the review shall leave no sting.

Ay, if in winding the labyrinth back,
Either glimmer on his track,
He then will prize it as a boon,
As cheering as the sun at noon.

And when in age midst youthful mirth,
With placid aspect on the hearth,
He musing sits the winter eves,
And so the tedium relieves,

His mien is often deemed serene,
Because of the entrancing scene,
When, on another fixed his gaze,
That smoothed his brow, of other days.

And when he through some byway lone,
A ramble takes, as age is prone,
Or in the street among the throng,
He threads his way, as lone, along:

On every friend that he may meet,
He seems to smile with joy replete,
When 'tis, perhaps, with a gladdening ray
His visage beams of another day.

Then if one were a boon indeed,
Whithersoever his pathway lead,
Smooth or rough, in weal or woe,
Throughout his journey here below,

O, what a favor! to be lent
The heavenly three in glory blent,
When he the shadowy vale draws near,
And earthly lights all disappear!

TO THE MEMORY OF J. B. M.

A tiny bud, our infant boy
   Was likened unto by the rest;
And of the rest the pride and joy,
   As he lay in his cradle, dressed.

And as a bud he then was nourished,
   The sweetest one of all the group;
And like the rest he grew and flourished,
   Yet anon appeared to droop.

And so, perhaps, because more rare
   Than other flowers on the bed,
It fell, despite our anxious care;
   The tiny bud, our boy, is dead.

He in his little casket lay,
   As all the rest around him wept;
And looked the weary child of play
   That in its cradle soundly slept.

While tolled the Village bells, the knell
   Of life departed, mournfully,
The earth upon his coffin fell,
   And gone, forever gone, was he.

The solemn rites came to a close,
   As Hesper peered through twilight gloom;
The wan moon in the heavens rose
   And shimmered on our Johnnie's tomb.

NEAR THE SHORE.

My voyage on a troubled sea,
   I mind, is nearly o'er;
My bark is drifting toward the lee,
   And drawing near the shore.
My castles that seemed firm in youth,
   Proving in age unsound,
Without oft stirring others' ruth,
   Have fallen to the ground.

I have full many a hopeful scheme
   Of happiness devised,
That ended like a midnight dream,
   At morn unrealized.
Yet have I drank of joy's sweet cup,
   In sparkling overflow;
Though when I quaffed the nectar up,
   The lees I found below.

In lucubrations often foiled
   Some erring soul to mend;
In many a tale have vainly toiled,
   A moral to append.
The lights along my path are fled!
   Still now and then, in dreams,
A spark, by smouldering embers fed,
   Appears in fitful gleams,

Lit by whose gladdening, gleaming rays,
    My steps I oft retrace
To olden scenes of other days,
    That hallow time and place.
And while upon that beaten track,
    As reveries come o'er me,
In its light they all come back,
    And mirrored are before me.

Whom are no more, therein appear,
    And we together mingle,
Converse hold, and sometimes here
    The scene is, at mine ingle.
The lost return unchanged by time!
    Yet change occurs in kind,
And age transmuted into prime,
    Beside my hearth I find.

In this retreat, like scenes among,
    O may I cares elude,
And sing my songs till all are sung
    In peaceful quietude!
My voyage on a troubled sea,
    I mind, is nearly o'er;
My barque is drifting toward th' lee,
    And drawing near the shore.

MY CHILDHOOD'S OLD HOME IN THE VALLEY.

I was born when the yule-log upon the hearth lay,
    The foot of a mountain the place;
And from childhood to age now my well-trodden way,
    Through the vista of years can retrace.

Bell Mount, while forsaken, indelibly graved it
    With memories of joys it bestowed,
As in the Neshaminy mirrored, that laved it,
    And into the Delaware flowed.

But grief woke an echo at life's morning stage,
    That with all its joys through it blending,
Deserves at its close in its story a page,
    For restraint o'er them timely extending.

'Twas a midsummer day, brother Will had completed
    My sail-boat, and rapt in the dream
Of pleasure, therewith to the shade we retreated,
    Below a rude bridge of the stream;

Like dreamers appeared, in a chaise passing o'er it
    The consorts of new-wedded bliss,
When, a wail from the bride, on a zephyr that bore it,
    Resounded adown the abyss.

Their steed, taking fright, having dashed through the railing,
   Engulfed with the wreck was the groom;
But the bride, from it 'scaped, on the bridge stood bewailing
   His rigid, untimeous doom.

The nymphs of the mountain still answer her wail,
   And the mead echoes wake, which the swain
Still prolongs with his lay, that resounds in the gale,
   And the tempest repeats the refrain.

But years rolled away, and my childhood's old home,
   Through their lapse the possession of strangers;
Its primitive indwellers o'er the world roam,
   Or are freed of its evils and dangers.

And those, one of these left behind, so, at rest;
   By the wayside, two sisters and mother;
And here, like immunity, in the northwest,
   Have father and my youngest brother.

And still there remain half the links of the chain;
   Oh, Death! from thy sting awhile spare us,
For sorrow and pain, at thy coming again,
   May merciful Heaven prepare us!

And in the northwest, as the years away rolled,
   And the seasons in order returned,
The lesson they taught, that I was growing old,
   I timely and heedfully learned.

For the solaces Age dreams and prattles about,
   The Present now failing support,
Its joys dwindling down as the days are worn out,
   To the scenes of the Past I resort.

At the fount where I quaffed it, o'erflowing of yore,
   Led back by the spells that oft bind me,
Still joyance I sip on the old attic floor,
   'Mid the trinkets and toys left behind me.

Since when, notwithstanding a manly lad grown,
   O'er my way back, as then, am now led,
To my swing that still hangs on the elm, but alone,
   My poor little playmate is dead.

The whitewashed stone schoolhouse appears in my dreams,
   Whither meetly I then wend my way,
And the pedagogue whilom yet find, as it seems,
   At his post, with the rod bearing sway.

To a slab in the churchyard in season repair,
   To it find overgrown with wild roses,
And by its inscription discern it is where
   Dear Willie profoundly reposes.

To the willow, the emblem of sorrow, return,
   Balmy dew yet therefor it distils,
And I yet in the snow thread my way through the fern,
   To my traps on the forested hills.

On the shore of the mill-pond in springtide I yet
    Hear its murmuring waves ebb and flow,
And anon take a fish with the spear, hook or net,
    That I used for the end long ago.

*   *   *   *   *   *   *

As I mused in the night on like scenes,
    Time-honored, time-battered or perished,
Forsaken while yet in my teens,
    And Memory so fondly hath cherished:

I resolved on a pilgrimage with her,
    To quiet the tumult of doubt;
With her light that gleamed on our way thither,
    She pensively led me about.

A recognized few, fifty years
    Of the havoc of time had sustained:
If any change moved me to tears,
    They nor were disguised nor restrained.

With a sigh at my dear Mother's tomb,
    As a tribute they duly were tendered;
Wild flowers hung o'er it in bloom,
    And fragrant the air round it rendered.

The duty was sad, yet a pleasure
    I felt it to kneel at that shrine,
So sacred because of its treasure;
    And brood over days of lang syne.

Vanished days wakeful Memory called back,
  When a heedful and fond Mother blessed me;
Oft traced to the hay-rick my track,
  And found me asleep and caressed me.

Poor life's morning dream had come o'er me;
  And still in hers after mine fled,
I left the good Matron who bore me,
  With a flower that grew on her bed.

To the graves of my sisters I sped me,
  Where Memory 'mong scenes long concealed
From mine eyesight, again gently led me,
  And by her light to me revealed:

When we plucked the bloom of the heather,
  And played hide-and-seek in the wold,
And gambolled like lambs in spring weather,
  Let loose from the pale of the fold.

Lest an episode injure my story,
  Their virtues I dare not disclose;
As Phœbus declined in his glory,
  I left them unsung in repose:

For my forefathers' hearth, with its cheers
  By strangers doled out to be greeted;
And, doubtless, the smiles and the tears
  Of its joys and its sorrows repeated.

Fond Memory so cleaves to the mortal!
  So broods over scenes of the Past!
Angel-like of a fane at its portal,
  Guarding the flock to the last.

Bell Mount, as I left it, appearing,
  Its echoes my spirits did rally;
And comfort afforded, till nearing
  My childhood's old home in the valley.

A mantle of moss on it lay,
  That its charming image defaced;
And Time, in his rounds night and day,
  Was busily laying it waste.

While grists the old mill was yet grinding,
  Its water-wheel dripping outside it,
The boon was denied me of finding
  An undershot in it, supplied it.

Less than in my childhood appeared it,
  And also the meadow below it,
The stream with the rest, as I neared it,
  That now and then used to o'erflow it.

Abandoned the church to decay,
  The ivy was through its walls creeping;
The owl in dreams wore out the day,
  And the night in his watch o'er it keeping.

Its bell that to vespers the people
    Once tolled, and the new year in rung,
Having fallen along with its steeple,
    Lay broken the ruins among.

While wending my way thence, a strain
    Shrilly rang, like a hunter's horn tooting,
And list'ning, I heard the old fane,
    Resounding the lone owlet's hooting.

The schoolhouse had fallen, and ended
    The pedagogue's mission as well,
Which gently my muse with it blended,
    As I conned the wreck where it fell.

Wherein, lest a vow made be broken,
    I rummaged for recognized traces;
Not even the stones gave a token,
    The whitewash was worn off their faces.

To the cheer of mine host, by the river,
    I fled, sorely put to the rack;
Quoth he, "you have qualms of the liver,
    Whose cure is a cup of old sack."

But not while the bright nectar flowed,
    And wit was indulged in its flight,
Was relief from my vapors bestowed:
    Nor till philomel sang in the night.

There to nourish my strength did I bide,
   All alone at the close of the day,
Of the comfort of kindred denied:
   Pilgrim-like homeward plodding his way.

As I woke, in the glimmer and gleaming
   Of day, as it dawned in the sky,
With joys was my restless mind teeming,
   Of other days by-gone for aye.

Yet I rued that the still fleeting hours,
   Unnoted while dreaming them o'er:
Like dewdrops that fall from the flowers,
   They sweetened withal, were no more.

When the queen of Night peered through the gloom,
   By her light in the churchyard I wandered;
And leaning upon Willie's tomb:
   The phases of life with hers pondered.

My last and most tedious night ended,
   Mine host, with his blessing in need,
The stirrup for me condescended
   To hold, while I mounted my steed.

My sojournment came to a close,
   As the morn o'er the mountain was gleaming:
Whose summit I reached as arose
   Behind it, the sun brightly beaming.

On a rock, unforgotten, moss-grown,
    While with browse I my steed did regale:
Final leave took in this wise, alone,
    Of my childhood's old home in the vale:

The pheasant still drums in the thicket;
    The fish multiply in the waters;
And chirps at thine hearth-stone the cricket:
    But absent thy sons and thy daughters.

Since here, all save one, broken-hearted,
    A meet tribute to thee did pay:
Oh! how hath thy glory departed;
    How changed by the years rolled away!

No more every tear of each fount,
    Shall we shed, as we thee linger o'er:
No more hear the tongues of Bell Mount,
    As we wind down it, answer, no more.

Though I leave thee to never return,
    At mine ingle thy story will tell:
While I live, and the yule-log shall burn,
    Sweet home of my childhood, farewell.

THE FOLLOWING POEMS ARE

BY

MARION JULIET MITCHELL,

AND

APPEAR HEREIN AT THE REQUEST OF
HER FATHER.

POEMS

BY

MARION JULIET MITCHELL.

HOURS OF THE PAST.

When early friends from us have gone,
   And youthful days are fleeting fast,
We seem to tread life's way alone —
   And love to muse o'er pleasures past.

Earth once to us, like heaven seemed,
   With naught therein but joy and gladness.
But ah! we then but little dreamed
   Our joy might some day turn to sadness.

Sometimes amid the busy throng
   We hear some old familiar strain;
Perhaps the cadence of a song
   That seems to bring years back again.

But then the spell is quickly broken,
   For no dear face, that we have known,
With form and voice, can give some token,
   That Time has with us backward flown.

Like those to whom in desert lands,
  Some sudden mirage oft appears —
We seek in vain to clasp the hands
  Of those we loved in other years.

But in some quiet twilight hour,
  Or in the visions of the night,
We may those happy days live o'er,
  As Fancy takes her wayward flight.

Once more these rooms and halls resound
  With mirth and music, as before;
In mazy dances — floating round,
  Are forms we loved in days of yore.

How gladly would we cast aside,
  All present joys — could this scene last;
And say to Time: Oh! onward glide,
  We'll dwell forever in the Past.

But like a mist before the dawn,
  This lovely vision fades away,
Those well-remembered forms have gone,
  And we alone are left to-day.

But when we too shall be set free,
  And that time now may not be far,
May we, in heaven, the loved ones see,
  And may we find " The gates ajar."

A MODERN WEDDING.

The spacious church was lighted
   In splendor like the sun ;
Two hearts their vows had plighted,
   And soon would be made one.

And like the beauteous bowers
   Of some blithe fairy queen,
The walls were decked with flowers,
   In garlands bright and green.

Assembled there in waiting
   Were many young and fair,
Impatient for the mating
   Of that devoted pair.

Rare gems in many a cluster,
   Reflected back the light
With pure and sparkling lustre,
   On that eventful night.

Not long the throng had waited,
   In quiet order meet,
When, though somewhat belated,
   Arrangements to complete,

The bridal party entered,
  In fashion's latest style,
And on them all eyes centered,
  While passing down the aisle.

The mighty organ's pealing,
  Resounded through each arch,
As then was played with feeling
  The grand old "Wedding March."

But soon the music ended;
  Those thrilling strains had ceased;
And as the last notes blended,
  They stood before the priest.

The bride, with satin trailing,
  And orange-blossoms crowned,
With costly lace inveiling,
  Her form and face so round,

Stood like a piece of sculpture,
  But rivalling all art;
For underneath was culture
  And throbbings of a heart.

The groom, in finest raiment
  And of a stylish mien,
Seemed proud to be the claimant
  Of that most charming queen.

We gazed with admiration
  On that brightest scene of life;
But 'twas of short duration,
  Ere they were man and wife.

Then followed the "reception,"
  And the dear five hundred went,
And rich, beyond conception,
  Were the costly gifts they sent.

And, when the guests departed
  And that bright scene was o'er,
The wedded couple started
  For some far distant shore.

The world seemed fair before them,
  And sorrows were unknown;
The lamp of Hope hung o'er them
  And with bright radiance shone.

But as our way we wended
  From scenes of joy so fair,
We thought how sometimes ended
  Bright castles in the air.

MY GRANDMOTHER'S HOME.

Within a valley, bright and green,
With landscape fair as e'er was seen,
That ancient mansion still remains;
But now, alas! its beauty wanes.

It stands a distance short apart
From the noisy din of a busy mart,
While not far off, the Genesee
Goes rolling on to its destiny.

Surrounded by those grand old trees
That caught the morning's earliest breeze,
I seem to see, in memory's light,
That dear old home, so fair and white.

The garden, with its luscious fruit
That could the most fastidious suit,
Was ever open, free to all—
And no one need to scale the wall.

In childhood's happy, sunny hours,
When earth appeared a field of flowers,
And underneath the sky so blue,
I not a care or sorrow knew:

How often through those haunts I strayed,
With naught to harm or make afraid,
And spent the days, from morn till night,
In pure enjoyment and delight.

And when I heard of Eden old,
And of its splendors I was told,
I wondered if 'twere half so nice
As grandma's little paradise.

But long since, now, those days have passed,
And on those scenes I've looked my last;
For strangers roam amid those bowers,
And pluck the tempting fruits and flowers.

The dear ones have all passed away,
And in a higher Eden stray:
But clearly I can see each face,
And in my heart they have a place.

Sometimes in dreams, I wander o'er
Those rooms and spacious grounds, once more;
Again the loved ones I behold
And hear their voices, as of old.

The scenes of childhood all return
And seem the wheels of Time to spurn
But this is all a passing gleam,
And soon I find it's but a dream.

From early scenes we drift away,
And farther we are borne each day;
And though we oft may turn our gaze
To catch the light of other days,

We find, ere long, we've gone too far,
And, like the glimmering of a star,
The light grows fainter on our route
Until at last its gleams die out.

AN EVENING SCENE.

The sun in his glory had sunk in the west,
And man from his labors was taking a rest;
The children had ceased from their sports for the day,
And yet in their dreams they were still at their play;
The shadows of twilight were creeping along,
And robins were singing their sweet evening song.

I sat by my window and felt the cool breeze
That came to me fresh from the fruit-laden trees,
The trickling of fountains I heard in the air,
And the murmuring voices of those young and fair;
And now, with new splendor to add to the scene,
The moon had arisen with silvery sheen.

From afar on the lake came floating the song
Of the boatmen, who sang as they glided along;
And, wafted with strains of the music around,
Came the fragrance of flowers that covered the ground.
I thought as I turned from that scene with a sigh,
It might be a glimpse of "the sweet by-and-by."

'Twas a scene that no painter could ever design,
And I, in my writing, shall fail to define;
But often in memory its beauties arise,
Like some lovely vision it seems to my eyes,
And long as this life with its powers shall last,
That scene will come back in my dreams of the Past.

ACROSTIC.

May, once more, with beauty crowned,
Yields her flowers to strew the ground;
Dewdrops glisten in early morn,
Each little flower and leaf to adorn;
All day long, in the trees so gay,
Robins are singing the hours away.

Faintly we hear, 'mid the songs of birds,
Afar in the fields the lowing of herds;
Thither the children repair in their play,
Happy to be from their lessons away;
Everywhere beauty and wealth doth abound,
Radiant sunshine is streaming around.

POETIC PURITY.

Far from the busy scenes of life
And all its endless cares and strife
   That weigh upon the mind,
The poet loves to steal away,
In some secluded haunt to stray,
   And leave the world behind.

In nature's paths, so wild and still,
His fancy then may soar at will
   Above the world's alloy;
He catches there the radiant gleams
That float from out the land of dreams,
   And fill his soul with joy.

He seeks for gems of beauty and worth,
And lifts them out of the dross of earth,
   Bestowing on us the prize;
We see too much of moth and rust,
Our sight is dimmed with tears and dust,
   A jewel delights the eyes.

Oh, shame on those with hearts so vile,
Who would this gift of heaven defile
   With themes so black and dire;
Who drag from snowy heights above
The pure and shining robes of Love
   Far down in loathsome mire.

Their words are like the simoom's breath,
That brings not life and strength, but death,
  That wounds, but cannot heal;
Or like some insect, seeming fair,
That doth a gilded covering wear,
  Its poison to conceal.

THE STORY OF A LIFE.

In looking back along the years,
  When days went fleeting by so fast,
In memory oft one form appears,
  Whose life with clouds was overcast.

While in the cradle yet she lay,
  Her mother kind a summons heard
From One whose will she must obey,
  And went to Him she long had served.

This first great loss she little knew,
  Nor realized for some few years;
But Time rolled on, she older grew,
  And then she mourned with bitter tears.

We next behold her at her school,
    A quiet, thoughtful, studious child;
One who required no rigid rule,
    But only hints and precepts mild.

Among the thoughtless and the gay,
    She walked as one of different mold;
She seemed to care not for their play,
    And like a lamb without a fold.

Years passed away, and in due time
    This child a maiden fair, appeared;
And like a rose-bud in its prime,
    To true perfection she had neared.

And now for her it seemed were stored
    Some pleasure and enjoyment here,
For one whose worth her soul adored,
    Her hand would claim within the year.

But cruel Fate around her clung;
    And deep the shadows round her fell;
No joyful wedding-bells were rung,
    But softly tolled the funeral knell.

The manly form in yonder mound,
    A victim fell to hardships dire,
While on contested southern ground,
    He fought beneath the rebels' fire.

But she whose life is here portrayed,
  This last great grief could not endure;
And day by day we saw her fade,
  Like some frail lily, white and pure.

The heart whose courage never failed
  Through life-long sorrows, now was crushed;
And when by this last blow assailed,
  Its weary throbbings soon were hushed.

Again the bells were softly tolled;
  Again rare flowers, their perfume shed;
Together met the young and old,
  To weep around the honored dead.

Beneath the spreading willow's shade
  (For lovelier spot in vain we search),
This maiden's mortal form was laid,
  Within the shadow of the church.

But far above its gilded spire,
  And far beyond all earthly woes,
Her spirit joined the heavenly choir,
  And dwells with loved ones in repose.

TO BRITAIN'S NOBLE QUEEN.

Most noble Queen, to thee I send
    A tribute due to worth,
For at that altar all should bend,
    Of whatsoever birth.

Thou art not like the queens of yore,
    With scepter crimson stained ;
Who shamed the jewelled crowns they wore,
    While tumult with them reigned.

Beneath the robes of state, we know
    Thou hast a woman's heart,
That well can feel another's woe,
    For thou hast felt its smart.

Beside the dying form of him,
    In youth thy chosen mate,
The cup of grief, filled to its brim,
    Was given thee by Fate.

The bitter dregs she bade thee drink,
    Thy heart to thus prepare,
From lesser trials not to shrink,
    And those of others share.

Thy life with honors meet is crowned,
   Thy head with gems and gold;
Yet weary hours thy heart hath found,
   In dreams o'er days of old.

The noble Prince, thy consort dear,
   In memory long will live;
His virtues we could but revere,
   And rightful homage give.

With Him who reigns o'er countless realms,
   To mortals yet unknown,
Whose mighty power the mind o'erwhelms
   With awe before His throne:

The chosen ones, from earth set free,
   Are safe forevermore,
And there thy loved one waits for thee,
   On yonder Golden Shore.

Above the reach of sorrows keen,
   Beyond all earthly strife,
He now awaits thee, noble Queen,
   His true and faithful wife.

WAITING.

Sweet Childhood, with thy painted toys,
Oblivious of those fleeting joys,
O sing and sport, for soon, alas!
Those bright and joyous days will pass;
But wouldst thou know thy latent powers,
That slumber through those sunny hours,
In vain thou shalt inquire of Fate,
Full many a year yet thou must wait.

Ambitious gouth, with eager gaze,
Looks forward in those halcyon days,
To laurels bright he hopes to gain,
But long he struggles for in vain;
Like mirage oft before his eyes,
Appears the goal and envied prize;
He still pursues the alluring bait,
But ere he grasps it, long must wait.

Matured Manhood, with like zest,
Pursues his phantoms with the rest;
But with more obstacles he copes,
Though not less ardent are his hopes.
Advancing years new trials bring,
While older ones around him cling;
With life alone these terminate,
But for deliverance he must wait.

Old Age with snowy locks appears
Beneath his weight of cares and years.
Subdued are now ambition's fires,
And higher hopes his soul inspires.
Almost within his eager gaze
Are dazzling gleams of heavenly rays;
And ere he sees the "Golden gate,"
He hath not now long yet to wait.

THE OLD HERMIT.

His home is in the forest deep,
  From worldly cares far, far away;
They neither can disturb his sleep,
  Nor vex and worry him by day.

Those grand old trees protection give,
  Alike from storms and summer's heat;
While on their leafy branches live,
  Myriads of tiny warblers sweet.

The squirrels leap from bough to bough,
  And boldly play around his door;
While deer and fawn, his favorites now,
  Roam fearlessly the ground all o'er.

He loves those scenes, so wild and fair,
    That art has failed yet to define;
He breathes that pure and fragrant air,
    With odors sweet, of cedar and pine.

But though that land is fair to view,
    And cares can ne'er invade that nook,
We query why—for scenes so new,
    He friends and all the world forsook.

The heart may oft a burden bear,
    Of which the world may never know;
The face, perchance, a smile will wear,
    While underneath is deepest woe.

In all his musings o'er the Past,
    And in his dreams of those once dear,
One fairy form from first to last
    He sees, and ever fancies near.

He sees a blue-eyed maiden fair,
    With love and pity in her eyes,
With whom he hoped his home to share,
    But now her home is in the skies.

In bridal robes she oft appears,
    Which she was once so soon to wear;
He seems to see, through blinding tears,
    The orange-blossoms in her hair.

And thus in dreaming o'er the Past,
  Or musing on what "might have been,"
The hermit's days will end at last,
  And may he join the loved one then.

O, why should we poor mortals here,
  Subjected be to ills so keen?
When we to earthly joys are near,
  Then cruel Fate steps in between.

Yet so our hearts are drawn while here,
  Away from earth and toward the skies,
To that eternal glorious sphere,
  Where there will be no severed ties.

PASSING AWAY.

The leaves of the trees are beginning to fall,
And out from the bushes the Katydids call,
The shadows of evening make haste to appear,
Thus we are reminded that autumn is near.
No longer the Robin is trilling his lay,
The beautiful summer is passing away.

The Reapers are busy, far out in the fields,
In gathering and storing what Earth richly yields.
With energy meet, they exert every power,
And while the day lasts they improve every hour.
They teach us the lesson, to work while we may,
Our season for labor is passing away.

As often we mingle amid the great throng,
We note the strange faces as we pass along.
How few of the number we see on the street,
Are those, in days past, we delighted to meet.
Another sad lesson we learn day by day,
The friends of our youth are fast passing away.

May some rays of sunshine yet linger around,
And summer's deep warmth in our hearts still be found;
And may the few loved ones we have with us yet,
Remain with us long — and our cares we'll forget.
Then when comes the summons we all must obey,
May we meet where the joys are ne'er passing away.

A REVERY.

Our thoughts are prone to wander back,
And travel o'er the beaten track,
'Mid scenes that will in memory live,
So long as life can reason give;
And through those years, that fled so fast,
In mazy labyrinths of the Past.

But in the Present we must live;
And take whatever Fate may give.
Sometimes, perchance, it will be joy,
But mingled with what will annoy:
And though our lot be good or ill,
Faith tells us 'tis the Master's will.

Our musings oft may cause a sigh,
As we review the days gone by;
But when we toward the Future look,
We seldom are by Hope forsook.
Her lamp is ever burning bright,
And will illume the darkest night.

When Time with us shall be no more,
And we are safe on yonder shore,—
The burdens we are bearing here,
Can ne'er invade that heavenly sphere,—
May Faith and Hope our guardians be,
And guide us o'er life's troubled sea.

TO MY FATHER ON HIS EIGHTIETH BIRTHDAY.

Dear Father, once again we hear
    The chime of Christmas bells;
And to our ears, their tones so clear,
    A tale of interest tells.

The story they have often sung —
    How on that night of glee,
When stockings by the chimney hung,
    In eighteen hundred three,

A tiny babe the children found
    With wonder and dismay;
In snowy raiment, sleeping sound,
    It in the cradle lay.

As now we look upon thy brow,
    In age serene and mild,
'Tis hard to realize that thou
    Wast then that little child.

In varied phases of this life —
    Like other pilgrims here,
Thou hadst thy share of cares and strife,
    Throughout thy long career.

Dame Fortune hath upon thee smiled,
  Though for a time she frowned;
In trouble, thou the time beguiled
  In studies most profound.

Thus wisely thou the time employed
  To learn the "Healing art";
That thou the boon thyself enjoyed,
  To others might impart.

And when thy "Parchment"—nobly earned—
  Thou didst in time receive,
Thy steps from early scenes were turned,
  Thy fortune to retrieve.

And in this genial western clime,
  Where then the red man reigned,
Thy home was reared when in thy prime,
  And here thou hast remained.

Thy faithful wife, and children three,
  In all these scenes have shared;
But one sweet babe was soon set free,
  And many evils spared.

And now, with many blessings crowned,
  Thy worldly loss restored,
May hope fulfilled to peace redound,
  And comfort meet afford.

May many a quiet, happy year
   By thee yet be enjoyed,
Till in a higher, better sphere
   Thy soul shall be employed.

THE VILLAGE CHURCH.

That sacred spot we can ne'er forget,
   And though long years since then have passed,
Those vineclad walls are standing yet
   As firm as when we saw them last.

We've looked on many taller spires,
   Heard priests who spoke in the Latin tongue;
The chanting heard of finer choirs,
   While the tones of grand old organs rung.

But though this world we wander o'er,
   Go where we will, in vain we search;
For scenes so quaint we'll see no more
   As those around the Village Church.

The rusty bell hangs in the tower,
   And still its clanging tones are heard
Calling the flock at the appointed hour,
   By custom fixed, to hear the Word.

The older ones and deacons grave
   Are early seated in their pews,
While younger members, time to save,
   Wait round the door to hear the news.

But when they dare no longer stay,
   For soon the "meeting" will begin,
They slowly tear themselves away,
   And now we see them going in.

The girls are decked in gay attire,
   And glad to show their bonnets new,
Which "city folks" might not admire,
   Though trimmed with ribbons, pink and blue.

The boys in home-made suits appear,
   Of which they seem to be quite proud,
Perhaps the style is a little queer,
   But this we must not say aloud.

The Parson, prim with rural grace,
   And hat in hand, walks down the aisle,
And when we see that solemn face
   We feel 'twould be a sin to smile.

Behind the desk he takes his stand,
   The walls with prayer and praise resound,
Then he his sermon takes in hand,
   Which he begins with look profound.

He tells his trembling hearers how
    The gates below are yawning wide,
And they their ways must alter now,
    Or they will some time there abide.

For these were times before the day
    When Ingersoll outran his sires,
And, being familiar with the way,
    Extinguished all the infernal fires.

But now the Parson's book is closed,
    His duties done and sermons ended;
Though some, perhaps, have through them dozed,
    Yet many more their ways have mended.

So ends our dream of rural life,
    And as its scenes fade from our view
We turn to worldly cares and strife,
    And bid the Village Church adieu.

OLD MUSIC.

Faintly, from afar, is ringing
   Ever in my listening ears,
Sounds of voices sweetly singing,
   Floating through departed years.

Soft and low, the tones are blended
   In each well remembered strain;
And, though long ago they ended,
   Still I hear the sweet refrain.

Though the voices of the singers
   May be heard on earth no more,
In my heart their memory lingers,
   There to dwell forevermore.

We are sometimes told by Sages,
   As to them it doth appear,
That re-echoed on through ages
   Are the words we utter here.

So, to me, it seemeth ever
   Are the songs I used to love
Floating on, and on, forever,
   Through the starry realms above.

TO LITTLE MAY McC.

(OF CHICAGO.)

Baby, with the curly hair,
   And happy, bright and laughing eyes,
How often does thy face, so fair,
   Before me, like a vision, rise!

I seem to see thee, as thou looked
   When in that handsome "Alcove-room,"
In snowy cambric, frilled and tucked,
   As sweet a bud as e'er did bloom.

I long to hear thy baby-talk,
   As now thy second summer dawns,
And watch thy timid, wavering walk,
   When thou art playing on the lawns.

The road is rough, and may be long,
   Thy little feet will have to tread;
And oft, amid the busy throng,
   Thy footsteps, doubtless, will be led.

But through all dangers that arise,
   That may annoy, and oft alarm,
May One above, who is all-wise,
   Protect and keep thee from all harm.

And may thy bark so smoothly glide
   Along the stream, till life is o'er,
That all the storms it will outride
   And land thee on the heavenly shore.

THE RETURN OF THE ROBIN.

Welcome, joyous little bird,
   From thy wanderings, far away.
Long it seems since we have heard
   The trilling of thy cheerful lay.

Why such haste in thy returning,
   While the ground is white with snow?
In our grates the fires are burning,
   Where wilt thou for shelter go?

Hast thou hastened back to tell us,
   Of the wonders thou hast seen?
Or to know what woes befell us,
   While long distance laid between?

Gladly we would hear thy story,
   Of that fragrant, sunny land,
Where the groves are crowned with glory,
   And by ocean breezes fanned.

But alas! in vain we seek
   Thy noisy prate to comprehend,
It only seems to us but "Greek"
   From beginning to the end.

Yet chatter on, thou happy bird,
   Thou art the harbinger of spring;
And when thy cheery voice is heard,
   All nature doth with welcome ring.

And, though Winter 'round us lingers,
   As if loath to yet depart,
Spring will loose his icy fingers,
   And soon will melt his stony heart.

Then from buds and blossoms springing,
   Warmed by breezes from the south,
Luscious fruit we'll soon be bringing,
   To fill thy little gaping mouth.

THE DYING CHILD.

A mother sat beside her child,
   With pallid cheek and anxious eye;
For as he lay with fever wild,
   She feared that he would surely die.

The feeble little hands she took,
   And caught each faintly uttered word;
With eager gaze she watched each look,
   But still no reason saw nor heard.

Her fainting heart was still sustained,
   With hope that reason might return,
And that while yet some life remained,
   He might his mother's face discern.

But hour after hour passed,
   And slowly wore the night away;
And now his life seemed ebbing fast,
   But still unconscious yet he lay.

With fever's deeply tinted hue,
   His lovely face had long been flushed;
But now was pale, and paler grew,
   And soon his moanings would be hushed.

As oft the dying ember shows
    A gleam of its departing fires;
And on surrounding objects glows,
    With brighter light as it expires.

So oft the soul, ere it departs,
    Emits a gladdening ray of light,
On sorrowing ones whose breaking hearts,
    Await in grief its final flight.

As now the mother sat beside
    Her child, and held his hand the while,
The deep blue eyes were opened wide,
    The sweet lips parted with a smile.

"Dear mother, can you see," he said,
    "That light that shines so bright around?
They told me little 'Sis' was dead,
    When she was buried in the ground;

"But now I see her right up there!
    With shining angels flying round;
I know her by her curly hair,
    My little sister I have found.

"She's calling me and I must go!
    Dear mother, now let go my hand;
I'll wear a dress as white as snow,
    And join that pretty angel-band."

And so the blue eyes closed again,
  To open here on earth no more;
And angels waited not in vain,
  To guide him to the "Heavenly Shore."

OLD OCEAN.

I listened to the tempest's roar
While standing near thy pebbly shore,
And thought how many loved ones sleep
Beneath thy briny waters deep.

How many, trusting in thy might,
Were lost forever from our sight,
And, when no arm was near to save,
Were dragged to some sea-monster's cave.

Unheard amid thy fearful gales
Are many a victim's dying wails,
And far beneath thy tossing waves
They find their dark and unknown graves.

But 'neath thine awful grandeur lies,
Deeply hidden from human eyes,
Many a pearl and sparkling gem
That well might grace a diadem.

Thy coral, with its tinted sprays,
Many a beauteous form displays,
And in the depths of thy bright shells
'Tis said that many a peri dwells.

Though like a tyrant thou dost reign,
And many an innocent is slain,
Within thy realm are beauties seen,
Unknown yet to earth's proudest Queen.

SOMEBODY.

The snug little parlor was lighted,
  A bright fire burned in the grate;
We knew there were vows being plighted,
  For somebody tarried so late.

A zealous young swain in yon bower,
  Unmindful of others' rude jeers,
Sings sweetly, though late is the hour,
  To somebody's listening ears.

From yonder high window a light
  Gleams out by a small taper fed;
And there we know, night after night,
  Is somebody toiling for bread.

We oft hear the merry sweet chime,
  Of church bells resounding so clear,
And know the appointed glad time
  For somebody's wedding is near.

Again the faint sound of a bell
  Comes wafted in tones soft and low;
And sadly its story doth tell
  Of somebody's partings and woe.

Thus often unheeded around,
  Life's cares so our time doth employ,
Are signs that with meaning abound,
  Of somebody's sorrow or joy.

ACROSTICS.

From all the outer world secure,
And scenes that others oft allure,
The student to his study goes,
Hither bent to find repose.
Ever patiently he toils,
Reams of paper though he spoils.

Matrons try with anxious care,
Oft for others to prepare,
Through their skill, those dainties sweet,
Having made, are such a treat;
Ever hoping they may find,
Rest from labor and of mind.

Winter's storms of sleet and snow,
In their might and fury blow.
Lawyers rest their wearied powers;
Lengthened are the evening hours;
In our homes, though, snug and warm,
All are safe from cold and harm,
'Mid the raging of the storm.

Cheering sounds now float about,
Heard above the storm without,
As the cello's thrilling tones
Rise above the wintry moans.
Loud, then soft, its notes now play,
E'en as lights and shades of day
Slowly pass at length away.

Ever mingling with the strain,
Linked as by a hidden chain,
On the evening air there floats,
Uniting all, piano's notes.
In harmonious strains they flow,
Soft as summer breezes blow,
Ere come winter's frost and snow.

Musing on the scene around,
A maiden sat, in thought profound;
Resolving then, should naught prevent,
Induced by love, if strength be lent,
On some fine day, and in due time,
Nimbly this scene to dress in rhyme.

www.ingramcontent.com/pod-product-compliance
Lightning Source LLC
Chambersburg PA
CBHW031748230426
43669CB00007B/542